THE BUSINESS LEGAL LIFECYCLE

How to Successfully Navigate Your Way from Start Up to Success

US EDITION

JEREMY STRETEN

First published by Jeremy Streten in 2019

ISBN: 978-1-925921-20-5 (pbk.)
978-1-925921-21-2 (ebk.)

Editing by Michael Hanrahan Publishing
Cover design by Designerbility
Layout by Michael Hanrahan Publishing
ebook by Michael Hanrahan Publishing

This book is available in print and ebook formats.

For Abigail and Benjamin

Disclaimer

(a) This information was not provided to suit any specific circumstances and is general in nature only. You acknowledge that you must make your own enquiries to determine the validity and appropriateness of the information provided herein.

(b) This information is not designed to provide, and is not to be substituted for, legal advice and other professional advice.

(c) Never disregard legal or professional advice, or delay in seeking it, because of the provision of this information. Never rely on any information we provide in place of seeking professional legal advice. You should also ask your attorney or other professional advisors to assist you in interpreting any information we provide, or in applying the information to your individual circumstances.

Contents

Foreword

May 28th, 1979 was a very important date for me – it was the opening day of my first business. Well, that was 14 businesses ago, and what an adventure it has been. Mustering up the courage to pull the trigger was tough enough, and without an ample supply of grit, determination and loads of perseverance this would have been an impossible task. Hindsight reveals self-employment and entrepreneurialism was no doubt the right choice, but no one told me how difficult it was going to be. Had they, I may still be someone else's top executive. I'm thrilled that everyone remained silent.

As I traveled through the various stages of business I was fortunate to have wise counsel. I was a magnet for mentors; maybe it was because wiser businessmen felt sorry for me and they witnessed the errors of my ways first hand. Or possibly my willingness to subject myself to the scrutiny of others gave them permission to guide me. I'm to this day not certain the reason but am nonetheless grateful for their openness.

What if I had a copy of *The Business Legal Lifecycle* by my friend Jeremy? I can't even imagine where I could be today. There were so many hurdles to overcome in the early days when I was so green at every turn. There were so many unanswered questions about my team, the name, structures, mission, vision, and values. Let me be honest: I wasn't even sure how to go about selecting a name. And, when I did select a name, what was I to do to protect it legally? There were so many fears creeping into my mind as it related to the best type of insurance, what would be employees' and managers' roles and responsibilities, and many other issues. It was almost debilitating.

A colleague suggested one day that I get legal representation, possibly even hire a law firm on retainer. This was a daunting challenge because until this point in my life I had no reason for legal input or representation. The truth of the matter was I was grinding it out day and night, attempting to make all the right decisions on my own. I didn't even know where to begin, and furthermore who could I trust? What would they charge, and how would I know what was fair to pay? Once I did select an attorney, I was always nervous to call. The receptionist always had the same response, 'He will call you back at his earliest convenience.' I truly believe I never got him on the phone one time the first go around. What's up with that? I needed him then.

What a goldmine of information is in this book, *The Business Legal Lifecycle*. Jeremy walks you through the various stages of business just at the right time.

He helps you through very important decisions like borrowing money, leasing your space, and the difficulties of insurance of various types. In the early days, I had no one to explain how to involve investors and explain the benefits or consequences. The list goes on and on as to the value of this book. There are suggestions and comprehensive plans as to how best to operate your business from a legal perspective.

At some point, I started thinking about selling my businesses and retiring, but I didn't know where to start. There were so many facets to selling: Was it a stock sale or asset sale? Was it all cash or earnout? How did I structure the deal to maximize the tax benefits and protect my estate? Was I solvent or could I be facing bankruptcy? Where was my guide, teacher and instructor to help with all these important questions? Well, here is the solution: The Business Legal Lifecycle.

Bottom line, I strongly suggest you take the time to read this thoroughly thought out strategic mindmap of how to operate a successful business legally.

Aaron Walker
Author of *View From The Top*

Preface

As an attorney and a business owner I am often frustrated with the legal industry as a whole. All too often, advice from attorneys is boring and repetitive with no thought for the client's actual situation. What happens more often than not is that clients are scared of going to their attorney, scared of being told that they need to spend tens of thousands of dollars to do everything that they need to do. There is no commercial advice given and legal advice becomes unworkable in the real world. This frustration led to the creation of the Business Legal Lifecycle, a concept to shift legal advice away from the simple 'do everything at once' approach to a more commercial set of instructions for every business owner to use.

This book is all about demystifying the legal processes and unlocking the often confusing world of legal advice for business owners. My aim is to give business owners a reference guide to be able to use in business, to give guidance on legal terms, and to give a clear direction of where a business is and should be going. The 13 phases of the Business Legal Lifecycle have been developed to solve these issues and give business owners a clear path for their business.

I originally wrote this book for the Australian market. I have worked with Keathel Chauncey and the team at Fresh Legal Perspective PL to help me adapt the concepts and theories to the laws of the United States. I could not have done this without your hard work and guidance, and am forever indebted to you for your assistance.

As with anything in life, business owners are on a journey of discovery. In writing this book, I have developed a deeper understanding of the Business Legal Lifecycle in general and discovered new and interesting ways to look at businesses. The examples I have given are designed to give that clarity to business owners to be able to identify whether they have encountered a similar problem in the past or as a beacon saying to a business owner that they are not alone and that issues that they face in business are normal. Moreover, I want to give you the knowledge and confidence to tackle problems head on and know that other business owners have been there before and there is always light at the end of the tunnel.

In writing this book I have researched other business books and legal processes and have also undertaken an extensive review of the business owners that I have dealt with over the years. I have examined where businesses did things correctly and where they did not, and I have developed the phases of the Business Legal Lifecycle as a guide to where the most successful businesses did things correctly.

Your journey as a business owner will be fraught with danger but it should be a journey that is interesting and allows you to develop many different skills.

Whether you are a small, medium or large business owner, you will at some stage of your business life have many different roles; embrace them and learn from your mistakes and also from your successes. This book has been designed for you to establish and build a successful business.

Introduction

Business owners are in business to take control

When you first start out in business, you need to do everything yourself to keep your business going. You need to be the marketer, strategist, salesperson, manager and even the cleaner. Staying in control of all aspects of your business is vitally important to its ongoing success. As your business grows and develops, it is critical that you are aware of the changes and cycles that it will go through. All businesses go through very predictable and repetitive cycles that are both positive and negative. They are all very important and you need to be proactive and ready to take action when the time comes. I have examined not only what successful business owners have done well, but also where business owners have failed, in order to work out what went wrong. This led me to develop the 'Business Legal Lifecycle' based on my experiences as an attorney working with over 5200 business owners and their businesses.

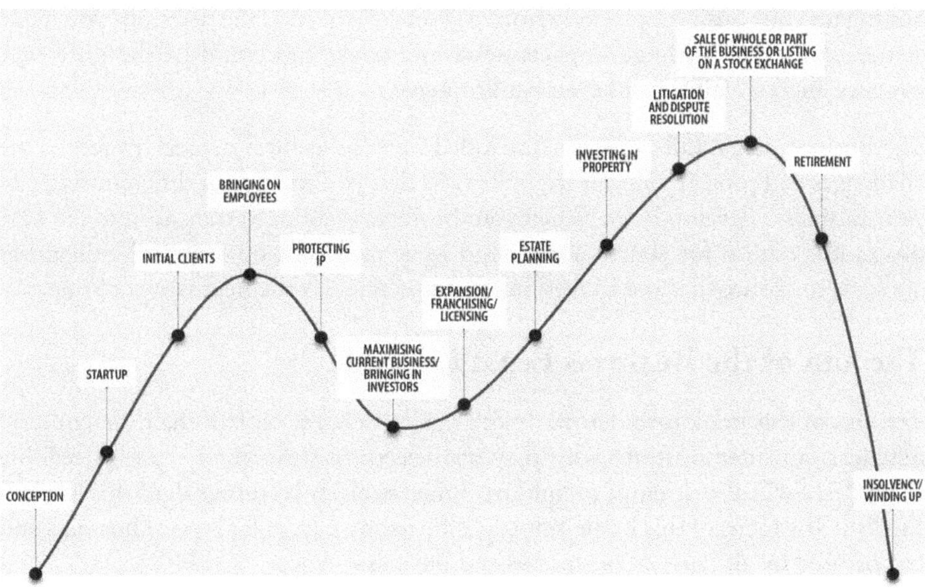

The main problem I observe is that many business owners don't know what they need to do with regards to the legal side of their business. They often don't establish the appropriate structure for their business and do not know when certain legal processes of the business should be undertaken. I developed the Business Legal

Lifecycle to guide businesses through what legal steps they need to take and when they need to take them.

Experiences

As a young corporate attorney during the 2000s it was drilled into me that a business should have every single legal document in place before it starts to trade. Part of this is due to the increasingly litigious nature of our society, and part is due to the commercialization of legal businesses.

Crossing the t's and dotting the i's before you start trading is critical in order to make sure that you are ready for the challenges that you will face as a business owner.

What we see from many business owners

All too often, a business owner, struggling to get their product off the ground, engages with clients and starts employing a team without having the resources or the time to implement all the necessary steps at the beginning of their journey. Setting up your business properly from day one is crucial as the decisions you make at the start will have huge impacts down the track, and could be the difference between success, failure and even bankruptcy.

The Business Legal Lifecycle was developed to help business owners overcome the challenges and protect yourself from the risks that you will face at different stages of your business's development. When your business is about to transition to the next phase, it is critical for you to understand what your legal options and obligations are so as to ensure that the transition from one stage to the next is successful.

The aim of the Business Legal Lifecycle

The aim of this book is to demystify the legal processes, explain the different legal practices, and demonstrate why they are necessary through the use of real-life examples. I will also attempt to fight my inner attorney by doing all of this in plain English! The focus of this book is not specific to any particular type of business and can be used by all types of businesses and business owners.

It should be used by entrepreneurs, existing business owners, accountants, attorneys, financial planners, business mentors, business coaches, mortgage brokers, business brokers, real estate agents and other professionals as a guide to the legal aspects of a business.

It may be that some steps occur in a different order or certain events trigger the phases slightly differently, but from my experience, both as a business owner and as an attorney, successful businesses generally follow a predictable pattern as presented in the Business Legal Lifecycle.

How to use this book

Before we begin, a word of warning: specific businesses and business owners have requirements that are unique to their particular circumstances. This book is a general discussion on the phases of the Business Legal Lifecycle, but it should not replace the advice that you, as a business or business owner, receive from your professional team of advisors which is specific to your own particular circumstances.

I have included many different case studies and examples to show how following the phases in the Business Legal Lifecycle can help your business grow into an asset that can either be sold, passed on/inherited or be used as a lifestyle business (a business set up to fund your ideal lifestyle as opposed to a larger type business). I have not included any names and some of the details have been changed for privacy. The effect of what happened in each case study or example, whether it is positive or negative, is very real. Ideally, you should read this book from cover to cover at least once and I encourage you to flag chapters that are especially relevant to you and scribble notes as you go. You may discover things that you have done correctly (or incorrectly) and, as you reach each transition to a new phase in your business, I encourage you to continually revisit the book to ensure that you follow the correct processes and seek the appropriate advice from your consultants.

What is the Business Legal Lifecycle?

Starting a new business is an exciting venture for any entrepreneur. I know from my personal experience of starting three businesses that sometimes you get swept up in the excitement and resist getting bogged down in important, but let's face it, often boring, legal matters. There is a long list of considerations that a business owner needs to think about when starting a business, with initial start-up costs typically being the driving factor behind making decisions.

This is one of the reasons that the Business Legal Lifecycle was developed: to ensure that you are aware that you need to start thinking about implementing the different legal processes from the very beginning.

The different phases of the Business Legal Lifecycle are:

(a) Phase 1 - Conception

(b) Phase 2 - Start-Up

(c) Phase 3 - Initial Clients/Customers

(d) Phase 4 - Bringing on Employees

(e) Phase 5 - Protecting Intellectual Property

(f) Phase 6 - Maximizing your Business/Bringing in Investors

(g) Phase 7 - Expansion/Franchising/Licensing or Buying an Existing Business

(h) Phase 8 - Estate Planning

(i) Phase 9 - Investing in Property

(j) Phase 10 - Litigation and Dispute Resolution

(k) Phase 11 - Sale of Whole or Part of your Business or the Listing on a Stock Exchange

(l) Phase 12 - Retirement

(m) Phase 13 - Insolvency/Winding Up

Each phase of the Business Legal Lifecycle will have a different impact on your efficiency and profitability. Consequently, you may decide not to go through a particular phase, or another phase may present itself earlier for you. Your company may enter into litigation much earlier in its lifecycle, or you may decide to invest in property sooner than others typically do. Some business owners decide never to franchise their business.

The phases of the Business Legal Lifecycle were created as a general guide based on our experience in dealing with business owners and the stages we see them experience during the life of their business. Whether you follow the cycle exactly or not, the book is designed to give you an idea of where your business is currently situated and where it is headed.

A word on contracts

Throughout the book I use various terms that refer to a contract, such as: a company's articles, a lease, agreements with your team and so forth. These are all forms of contracts which are very important legal documents. There is an old saying in the legal profession, 'in any dispute there is your belief as to the truth, there is the other side's view on the truth and then the actual truth is somewhere in the middle.' This is especially true if you do not have a contract in writing as each party to the contract will have a different interpretation of the agreement. In the ever-increasingly litigious nature of our society, putting a contract in writing is imperative for any agreement so that all parties can agree upon the terms and conditions.

CHAPTER 1
Phase 1 – Conception

The initial phase in the Business Legal Lifecycle begins when you first have the idea for your business. Business coaches may call this phase 'Birth' or 'Courtship'. In essence, the Conception phase involves everything you need to consider before you actually start your business.

At this phase of your business, you are simply trying to breathe life into an idea. The phase is built on your enthusiasm and commitment to your idea for a new business, product or service. You need to satisfy a market need and determine if the new business, product or service is a viable offering. During this phase, funds are always at a premium and capital is scarce. You are often living day-to-day or week-to-week to make ends meet for your dream.

Important considerations during this phase are:

- Do I have a conceptually viable new business, product or service? What makes it viable?
- Is there a market for my business, product or service? How is my business, product or service better than what is already out there?
- Who needs my service? What kind of client am I looking for?
- How much is it going to cost to get through the Start-Up phase?
- How am I going to fund my business before I get to the Start-Up phase?
- Who will be my first customer or client?

Dangerous ways of thinking during this phase are:

- Having second thoughts about the business
- Examining the future without looking at the present
- Having an exclusive focus on making money with no foresight on what is necessary to build the business

Successfully navigating through the Conception phase from a legal perspective requires business acumen and the right advice. Obtaining the right information and advice early can save you thousands of dollars in costs and taxes in the future.

During this phase, I will discuss a number of elements that are important to you as an entrepreneur. These include putting together your initial team, setting business goals and creating the right business name and brand. I will also provide some examples where this phase has been successfully navigated by other business owners.

1.1 Your Initial Team

A trusted long-term client of mine once said to me that every business needs a good accountant to minimize your risk, a good attorney to ensure that your business is legally compliant, a good financial planner to guide you through the complexities of your finances, and a good banker or mortgage broker to ensure that you get the best deal for your loans.

This statement has always rung true for me. I have seen clients who have tried to obtain advice from as many people as possible or, worse yet, 'barbecue advice' from friends and relatives, resulting in disastrous consequences.

There is no 'one size fits all' solution when it comes to advice for entrepreneurs and business owners. Each business and business owner is unique and it is critical that you obtain advice from a small, trusted group of professional advisors to ensure that your own situation is properly considered. These sources should be sufficient to give you the advice that you need; however, they should be able to acknowledge when they have reached the limit of their usefulness and additional expert advisors are needed.

It is essential, as a minimum, that you obtain advice from an accountant and an attorney during the Conception phase of your business. If you do not, you are travelling blind through the opening phase of the Business Legal Lifecycle. I can assure you that a small investment of time and money during this phase will end up saving you thousands in the future.

Also keep in mind that you need the right third party consultant for the job. You need to interview the third party consultant, whether it be an attorney, accountant or other consultant, and make sure that they know what they are doing. By all means take recommendations from friends and family, but ensure that the third party consultant that you engage meets your requirements in terms of what you need from that person for your business.

1.2 Goals

During this phase it is also a good idea to start considering your goals for the business. What do you hope to achieve in five years' time? Where do you need to be at the three-year mark, the two-year mark, and the one-year mark to reach those goals? Setting clear, defined goals with manageable steps to reach them is a sure-fire way to ensure that your business will be a success. If you do not have any idea about where you are going, you are never going to get there. Ideally, as part of this process, you should draft a business plan to establish what you will need to do to achieve your goals.

As a business owner, you should also consider key financial documents such as cash flow projections (depending on the type of business, you may want to do this for 13, 26 or 52 weeks) as well as a first full year budget. I know from personal experience that when you set yourself a goal, not only is it a great motivator to help you actually achieve your goal, it is also a wonderful feeling when you accomplish it. This is the simplest way to get the business that you want and ultimately to live the life that you want to live.

1.3 Choosing the Right Name

In the process of developing your business through the Conception phase, you also need to consider what you are going to call your new business, product or service. Ultimately, it is a matter for you, and you should only use a name that you are comfortable with going forward. This is going to be the name by which all of your customers and clients will know your new business, product or service, and you need to ensure that it is catchy and memorable.

From the Case Files

I have seen a number of success stories where business owners put together the right team before they started their business. One such example was a client who bought a bicycle shop. This was an existing business that had been trading for a number of decades, but the owner wanted to retire and get out of the game. The client was not an experienced business person but wanted to build a successful business. He came to us seeking advice before he entered into the contract to purchase the business and we ensured that he had accounting and business strategy advice from the right team before he did anything else. This meant that from the outset, his business was set up correctly by having all of his consultants on the same page and the business could properly proceed to the next phase. It also potentially saved him thousands of dollars from going back and recreating what he should have done correctly right from the start. This client continues to operate a very successful business as a result of implementing the right steps at the Conception phase.

1.4 Conclusion

Unfortunately, the first three phases of the Business Legal Lifecycle (Conception, Start-Up and Initial Clients) are the phases that most business owners do not get right. The reason for this is a combination of trying to cut costs and save money, a lack of knowledge, and excitement about going into the market quickly.

Often business owners will only see their attorney once they have started to employ a team to help with their business. Unfortunately, this is often too late and problems that could have been avoided have started to manifest.

Successfully navigating your way through the Conception phase of the Business Legal Lifecycle is critically important to the long-term success of your business. Once you have conceived your idea, you should seek advice from your attorneys, accountants, financial planners, business mentors and coaches to ensure that you can successfully navigate your way through to the Start-Up phase.

Doing this ensures that you are on the right track to establish your own successful business by not rushing the crucial first steps and starting your business in the correct way.

QUESTIONS TO ASK BEFORE YOU PROGRESS TO THE NEXT PHASE:

1. Do you have a clear understanding of your new business, product or service?
2. Is the new business, product or service viable?
3. What is the market for the business, product or service?
4. Who are your ideal clients for the business?
5. Do you have the right team in place?
6. Who needs your service? What kind of client are you looking for?
7. How are you going to fund the Start-Up phase?

CHAPTER 2
Phase 2 – Start-Up

The Start-Up phase commences the moment you take the plunge and start your business. This may include setting up the entity to operate your business, signing a lease for your premises or borrowing money to invest in your business. If you have not successfully completed the Conception phase of the Business Legal Lifecycle, the Start-Up phase will be the scariest phase as you are not in control of all aspects of your business. Problems and pitfalls will pursue you on a daily basis and prevent you from getting to the next phase (Initial Clients).

Generally, a business in the Start-Up phase will be opportunity-driven and action-orientated as the business owner will react strongly to different ideas and pressures and try to be all things to all people at all times. You need to accept that, as a business owner, you will be constantly stressed during this phase. This is completely natural as you take your first steps into the business world without the 'safety net' of paid employment.

If you follow the Business Legal Lifecycle, then you can start up your business correctly which will save you a lot of money. After successfully navigating your way through the Conception phase, there are a number of matters you need to consider as the Start-Up phase has the most variables and options of all of the phases of the Business Legal Lifecycle.

Important considerations during this phase are:

- Setting up the correct structure for your business
- Creating your brand
- Funding your business until your first client is obtained and pays you for your services
- Defining your responsibilities
- Deciding where you are going to operate your business from
- Entering into a lease that is on commercial terms
- Managing crises

- Dealing with management issues without having management experience

Dangerous ways of thinking during this phase are:

- Rushing your new business, product or service to the market too quickly
- Trying to be all things to all people
- Not recognizing and accepting errors or mistakes
- Pushing on despite insufficient funds to cover the initial cash flow for the new business, product or service

During this phase I will discuss concepts such as structuring the ownership of your business, entering into a lease for the premises from which the business will operate, the director's responsibilities, considerations if you want to be a franchise, taking out loans, and insurance. While this seems like a lot to consider early on in the process, these steps are crucial in order to establish a business properly and to complete the Start-Up phase.

I have left out a number of aspects that are ordinarily recommended by attorneys as I want to focus on only the most essential elements needed to get your business off the ground at this cost-prohibitive stage. I can't emphasize strongly enough how critical it is to obtain advice from your key advisors (accountant, financial planner and attorney) on these issues.

Your goals and circumstances are unique to you, and there is no 'one size fits all' model. Anyone who tells you otherwise does not understand what is required to establish a successful business.

2.1 Structures

A structure is a separate legal entity to operate your business. It can be seen as the vehicle or entity that you are using to purchase or establish the new business, product or service. A structure may also refer to multiple vehicles or entities; for instance, a builder may set up one entity to run their construction company, another to own the assets of the business, another to own the real property assets that are being constructed, and one to operate a different business associated to the other vehicles or entities in the one structure.

Setting up the right structure for your business at the outset is crucial to its future. Often when clients first come to see me, they have been speaking to other people about setting up their business.

Unsurprisingly, they have decided that they want to 'set up shop' exactly the same way as their friend set up their business. While the advice may be accurate and sound – for the other business – it may not be right for you.

It is crucially important that you obtain independent advice from your advisors about the best structure that needs to be set up based on your unique circumstances. Key questions include:

- What is your current financial and personal situation?
- What structures, if any, do you have in place now?
- What liabilities do your current structures have and can this be used to your advantage in the new business?
- What assets do you own and in what structures?
- What are your long-term strategy and goals; that is, do you want to set up the business to earn an income and be a long-term lifestyle business, or do you want to build a business that you can sell once it is properly set up?
- What is your personal/family situation?
- Are there other unrelated investors from whom you need protection?

The biggest pushback that I see in this phase is when a business owner does a cost vs benefit analysis when setting up the correct structure. Whilst the initial start-up costs may seem high, they are essential to ensure that you:

- Protect any other assets that you own
- Consider your succession planning
- Effectively plan the best tax position for your business

From a legal perspective, each business, and where possible each different aspect of the business, should be a separate vehicle or entity under one overarching structure. This means that should one vehicle or entity fail, then your other vehicles or entities will be protected.

An attorney will only advise you as to the appropriate structure you need for your business from a legal perspective. You also need to obtain tax, accounting and financial advice before setting up the structure to ensure that you have carefully considered all aspects of your business before moving forward.

There are four different common structures that may be suitable for a new business. Which one you choose depends on your situation, your goals, and the model you have chosen. They are:

(a) sole proprietor

(b) corporation/company

(c) limited liability company

(d) partnership

Don't forget, when setting up a new business you must always evaluate the risks and consider future problems that may arise that are beyond your control. Setting up the right business structure during the Start-Up phase will save you a lot of money and grief down the track.

Sole proprietor

The term 'sole proprietor' refers to a business being operated by a person in their own name, for example Bob Smith trading as Smith's Auto Repair. Operating as a sole proprietor is the most common structure for small businesses in the United States. It often comes as a surprise to many business owners that by operating a business in their own name, they take primary responsibility for all debts and liabilities of the business. As the operator of the business, they are personally liable for any defective work, any injury caused through their business, and for all debts that the business incurs. From a legal perspective, starting a business as a sole proprietor carries the greatest risk.

You must always consider both the short-term and long-term problems associated with operating a business. Events and risks beyond your control may mean that you lose a lot of money in the future that could have been prevented if you set up the right structure in the first place.

From a legal standpoint, being a sole proprietor is an extremely risky way to operate a business. There are other structures that can better protect you and your assets, and minimize the tax payable for the profits from your business.

Corporation/Company

A corporation/company is a separate legal entity from the people behind the business; it 'shifts' the risk of liability in many circumstances away from the owners of the business to the corporation/company itself. There are many different types of corporations/companies that you can use in the United States. Each state has its own register of companies, with their own similar rules that vary from state to state. In this section I am giving you a general overview of corporations to give you a basic grounding in what you will need to consider. There is no 'one size fits all' approach, so you need to speak to your attorney and accountant to determine which type is right for you.

The three main roles in a corporation/company are directors, officers and shareholders. Directors oversee the corporation/company, appoint and supervise the officers, and are responsible for protecting the shareholders. Officers are the President (or CEO), Vice-President (or COO), Treasurer (or CFO), and Secretary. The people in these roles usually take decisions made by the board of directors and implement them into the day-to-day operations of the corporation/company. Officers each have different roles, and make decisions on procedural matters such as entering into contracts, paying wages, and a variety of other aspects of the business operated by the corporation/company. They are there to ensure that the business is operating profitably, and they also hold responsibility for a number of other aspects of the business: see the overview in section 2.3.

As part of their role, directors and officers may be held liable for debts incurred by the corporation/company. This generally only occurs if they sign a personal guarantee, or if they incur debts on behalf of the corporation/company when they know that the corporation/company is insolvent (more on this in section 13) or if the director or officer breaches their fiduciary duties (more on this in section 2.3). Shareholders, on the other hand, own the business according to the number of shares that they have in the corporation/company. Shareholders are said to have the real control of the business as a majority of shareholders (shareholders who own over 50% of the shares in the corporation/company) can appoint and remove directors from the corporation/company.

You may have heard the phrase, 'a $2 company'. This refers to the share capital of the corporation/company. The number of shares each shareholder buys, which can be paid up, or the money 'owed' to the corporation/company, generates the share capital. A shareholder's liability is limited to the amount they still owe for their shares. This means that if you start a corporation/company and buy 10 x $1 shares in that corporation/company, you are liable to pay the corporation/company $10, if you have not already paid. The only other situation where a shareholder will be liable is if a lender or supplier requires a personal guarantee from the shareholders of the corporation/company. This limited liability protects the shareholders from the debts of the corporation/company and means that creditors cannot pursue the shareholders for the debts of the corporation/company.

Corporation's/Company's Articles of Incorporation

Each corporation/company in the United States should have its own articles of incorporation, which essentially state the rules and regulations by which the company will operate. It governs the company's relationship with its shareholders and directors in a general sense and provides a framework for the management of the company.

Shareholders' agreement

A 'shareholders' agreement' is another type of contract between the shareholders that sets out rules in relation to the company's management. This agreement, albeit not compulsory, is generally more comprehensive than articles, and if used, must be drafted with the articles in mind to ensure that there is no conflict between the two documents. Where you have multiple shareholders it is important to consider the different roles that each shareholder performs, and to what extent they can make decisions and agreements that affect the other directors and shareholders. I will discuss the options of shareholders' agreements, and buy/sell option agreements, in sections 6.3 and 8.4.

Limited Liability Company

Operating a business through a limited liability company (LLC) is also very common in the United States. An LLC combines the flexible structure of a partnership (see below) with the benefit for its members of the limited liability of a company. An LLC owns the assets of the business and is liable for its own debts; and the members act as its agents and only have liability up to the amount they have contributed to the LLC. It is a separate legal entity from the members of the LLC and is a registered entity. If you choose to operate your business through an LLC then you need to make sure that you use the name and include the words 'LLC', 'llc' or 'limited liability company' after the name of the LLC.

An LLC structure is a hybrid legal entity that provides flexibly to business owners. The members of the company are not personally liable for the company's debts or liabilities while allowing the members to take advantage of flow-through taxation. An LLC will have its own articles of organization.

Partnership

A partnership is a structure whereby a number of vehicles or entities partner together to operate a new business, sell a product or service, or own an asset.

An un-incorporated partnership is used much less frequently these days due to the fact that the individual partners, as in a sole proprietor structure, remain primarily liable for the debts of the business. There is no separation between the business owner/s and the outside world contracting with the business.

To help shift liability to the entity, you can set up a partnership of trusts, companies or individuals. A partnership of trusts is a popular structure for accountants where their clients are investing in real property, as it has many advantages from a land tax perspective in the United States. Other forms of partnership include Limited Liability Partnership and Limited Liability Limited Partnership. Each of these is used in different circumstances, so you need to speak to your attorney and accountant to ensure that you use the correct entity for your situation.

The partnership agreement

Where entering into a partnership, it is critical that you have a properly constituted and drafted partnership agreement. Like the articles of a company, a partnership agreement sets out the rules governing the relationship between the partners, including defining responsibilities for the day-to-day operation of the business. It is also critically important to plan for the end of the partnership to give partners an appropriate 'exit strategy'.

Trading/business name

It is important that you register any trading or business name as required by your local laws. This will ensure that nobody else can use that name in competition with you. Also, some laws provide that you cannot trade a business without having it registered with the appropriate government body.

It is important to note that each state in the US has its own register of names. If a company registers a name only in Florida and a different company registers the same name only in Texas, both companies will have rights to the name. However, a trademark registered with the United States Patent and Trade Office (see section 5.1 below) will have nationwide protection.

Conclusion

It is common to have a variety of different entities or vehicles within your structure, allowing for the most tax-effective distribution of your income and capital of the business. There is no 'one size fits all' structure for a business.

When setting up a structure, it is essential that you seek complete advice from qualified professionals that caters to your unique situation. Therefore, be careful simply relying on 'friends and family' or 'barbecue' advice when it comes to making important and complex decisions about running your business.

2.2 Leasing Premises

A large number of businesses operate from commercial, industrial or retail premises, often owned by a third party landlord. The relationship between the business owner (the lessee/tenant) and the owner of the premises (the lessor/landlord) is important for the successful running of the business. Being able to effectively operate your business without interference from third parties such as landlords is important for the early success of a business.

As a business owner, you need to ensure that any lease you enter into is on fair commercial terms and is affordable. The exact commercial terms will depend on the premises being let and your particular circumstances. It is essential that you have advice from all of your consultants during the lease negotiations to ensure that you enter into a lease that is advantageous for you and your business.

Far too often I have had to help clients that didn't get timely advice and tried to do it all themselves. The first mistake they made was not realizing they were negotiating with a landlord and/or agent who dealt with these types of matters every day and were expert negotiators. Unless you get the right advice, you may very well find yourself agreeing to terms that will hurt your business down the track.

Important considerations when leasing premises include:

- The amount of rent and when it is payable
- The length of the lease and any options to renew at the end of the initial term. This is essential as you plan for the future
- Whether the rent includes outgoings and/or operating expenses. Outgoings are the expenses generally incurred by the landlord such as

rates, cleaning costs, rubbish removal, maintenance of air conditioning, lifts, escalators, security, repairs and maintenance, insurance premiums and management costs. Operating expenses are consumables generally incurred by the tenant such as electricity, water, gas and are dependent upon the tenant's consumption at the premises

- The type of security you need to provide to the landlord. This may include a bank guarantee, bond/deposit or a personal guarantee and will depend on the type of entity entering into the lease
- Whether there are any incentives, such as rent–free periods or build out contributions paid by the landlord, to induce you to enter into the lease

Commercial leases

It is important to ensure that a commercial lease properly reflects the agreement between the parties as there is no such thing as a standard commercial lease; each lease reflects the different terms and conditions negotiated between the parties.

The process for entering into a commercial lease is a complicated one and it is important that you understand all of the required steps prior to going through the process to ensure that nothing is overlooked.

The process is:

(a) Finding the property

(b) Initial negotiations

(c) Drawing up the lease

(d) Your obligations as an ongoing tenant

Finding the property

The first step in entering into a commercial lease is locating the property that you want to lease. The crucial element here is to find a property that meets your space and location requirements; these initial aspects of the search will help you to determine what commercial property is right for your business. The appropriate property for any business will vary greatly depending on the type of business, its target audience, the requirements of local authorities and the business owner. You need to speak to an appropriate commercial agent to determine all of these factors and find the right property for your business.

Initial negotiations

After you find the right premises you would ordinarily contact the letting agent or the owner if no agent is appointed. They will have a letter of offer or agreement to lease for you to complete and sign. This document usually contains the salient features required for the lease, including the name of the landlord and tenant, the rent and outgoings payable, the commencement date, the area of the premises, the length of the lease (with any options to renew), and any incentives that the landlord is offering you to enter into the lease.

It is essential at this point that you seek advice from your consultants, such as attorneys, accountants, financial planners and business mentors, to ensure that the terms are commercially suited for your business and there is nothing untoward in the letter of offer or agreement to lease such as a change that you did not agree to, or where it places an obligation on you to perform a task during the lease that is unusual or unreasonable.

Once you sign this offer or agreement to lease you are bound by the terms of the document. The documentation will usually require that you pay a deposit, which you will need to pay upon signing. If you are unable to obtain professional advice before signing, you should ensure that you read through the document carefully and ask that:

(a) It be subject to your attorney's approval; and

(b) That you be entitled to a full refund of any monies paid if you do not proceed with the lease.

The lease

Once you have agreed to the terms of the lease, the landlord will instruct their attorney to prepare the formal lease agreement. This document will set out the terms and conditions upon which you will lease the property.

At this point, if you have not previously engaged an attorney, it is essential that you do so now in order to ensure that all of your requirements are covered in the lease and that you are not left with any onerous requirements or terms to which you have previously agreed in the initial negotiations.

General provisions to be considered

Given that there is no standard commercial lease document, it is important to remember that the terms of a lease will be negotiated by the parties to ensure that they properly reflect the rights and obligations of each party and that the terms are not too onerous on either party, especially the business owner tenant.

There are various matters that you should consider in entering a lease. These include:

- The initial rent and the method for calculating the rental increases over the term of the lease
- The initial term and how the lease is to be renewed or extended
- Whether local town planning (zoning) laws allow your business to operate from the particular premises and under what conditions
- Your right to transfer or assign the lease if you decide to sell the business, and the expense of doing so
- Whether you can sublet the premises
- Who pays for:
    - keeping the premises in good repair including structural improvements
    - rates and taxes
    - outgoings and other charges
    - all the additions, improvements, and fixtures made during the lease
- The types of insurance required and who obtains each type of insurance
- Restrictions on the removal of fixtures and fittings
- Your obligation to remove partitions and reinstate the premises after expiry to its original condition
- The consequences of failing to pay rent
- Your right to end the lease before it expires
- The process of resolving any disputes with the landlord
- Whether any specific legislation applies to your lease and the obligations it places on each party

- Special obligations if you are in, for example, a business park, shopping mall or multi-story building
- Payment of a security deposit, bank guarantee and/or the terms of any personal guarantee

Obligations as an ongoing tenant

Too often, business owners do not maintain their obligations during the term of the lease which may have serious consequences for both the owner and the business. Some of the major areas in which I have seen business owners fail in maintaining their obligations as an ongoing tenant include failing to:

- Comply with the conditions of the lease and any rules set out by the landlord
- Give notice in time to renew the lease
- Understand their rights if they stay on as a tenant without renewing the lease
- Obtain the landlord's consent if they wish to change the type of business they run
- Understand the landlord's right to end the lease early

Before you take possession and undertake any works on leased premises you should take photos or a video of the premises as a record of the condition that the premises were in at the time you took possession. This is critical, because by the end of the lease, which may be three, five or 10 years after you take possession, a dispute may arise with the landlord as to the original state of the premises which is usually the level to which you have to reinstate the premises at the end of the lease. Photographic evidence from the start of the lease is the best evidence to ensure that you can comply with this requirement.

2.3 Directors' and Officers' Responsibilities

If you are a director or officer of a corporation/company, you need to be aware of the rules, regulations and responsibilities regarding those roles in the corporation/ company. This section is focused on the United States laws relating to directors' and officers' responsibilities. These general principles also apply in most of the countries that allow business owners to set up corporations/companies to operate their business.

Corporation/company directors and officers are subject to common law and statutory duties in the United States. These duties are designed to promote good governance of corporations/companies and ensure that directors and officers act in the interests of the corporation/company – including putting the corporation's/company's interests ahead of their own.

As mentioned earlier in section 2.1, one of the advantages, from a legal perspective, of a corporation/company structure is that a separate legal entity operates the business and, in most circumstances, protects the individuals behind the corporation/company from any personal liability.

However, abuse of this protection has seen unscrupulous directors and officers hide behind the corporation/company to incur debts that they know cannot be paid. The law has developed over time to protect third parties dealing with these unscrupulous directors and officers.

The two primary fiduciary duties of a director are:

(a) Duty of Care

A director is obliged to keep themselves properly and completely informed as to the company's affairs and cannot claim ignorance of their own making (e.g. failure to undertake proper enquiries). All decisions must be made from an informed position to ensure they are active in the decision making process. What this means in practice depends on the circumstances.

(b) Duty of Loyalty – The duty to act in the best interests of the company as a whole

A director will breach this obligation if they are found to have subjectively failed to give proper consideration to the company's interests as opposed to their own interests.

A number of defenses may be raised by directors to allegations of breaches of duties. For further advice on breaches of duties, I strongly recommend speaking to your attorney to discuss what actions should be taken to protect yourself.

2.4 Becoming a Franchisee

One option when starting a business is to purchase an existing business in the form of a franchise. This is distinct from the 'Expanding Your Business, Franchising and Licensing phase' (discussed in section 7) because, rather than starting up your own business and brand, you are purchasing an existing franchise. Usually, the franchise will have all of the aspects of the business already established, so when you buy a franchise you are also buying that system to operate your business.

What happens when you want to invest in a franchise?

To invest in a franchise, the franchisee (you) must first pay an initial fee for the rights to the business, training in the business model, and the equipment required to operate the franchise to the franchisor (owner). After the business is set up, the franchisee will generally pay the franchisor a regular royalty payment (such as a percentage of gross sales or fees) for the continued use of the franchise model. These payments are commonly to be made on a monthly or quarterly basis. When you buy a franchise you are effectively buying a brand that should be protected by a registered trademark and gives you the right to trade using that trademark.

After the franchise agreement has been signed, the franchisee will open a franchise business which replicates the business model of the franchisor. Generally, as a franchisee you will not have as much control over your business as you would over your own business, so you need to be prepared to do things the franchisor's way, not yours. Usually, the franchisor will assist the franchisee where necessary to ensure that the reputation of the business trademark and model are maintained.

Control of the franchise

Generally, the franchisor will require that the same business model is used by all the franchised businesses. This may include using the same uniforms, business processes, and signs or logos particular to the business itself. These help to identify the business and keep the brand consistent to the outside world. The franchisee should remember that they are not just buying the right to sell the franchisor's product, but the right to use the successful business process of the franchise.

Often the franchisee will pay an advertisement fee to the franchisor so that consistent advertising can be utilized to a larger audience rather than each franchisee attempting to advertise their business on their own. For example, a franchisee may only be able to afford to advertise in a limited area around their business due to the cost. Where multiple franchisees pool their money together, they can often afford advertising that reaches a much larger market and is therefore more beneficial to all of the franchisees as a whole.

While there are many benefits to investing in an already successful franchise business, there can also be drawbacks. As with any investment, you should do your research thoroughly before you make any purchasing decisions. Often, the franchisor will place a number of restrictions on how you operate the business and, as such, you should ensure that any franchise agreement is fully reviewed by a competent attorney who can advise you in relation to your rights and obligations under it. It is also critical that you obtain advice from your accountant and financial planner to ensure that you are able to properly operate the business from a financial standpoint.

Conclusion

Purchasing a franchise business is an important business decision. You need to give serious consideration to what you are signing up for and whether you are getting the most out of your investment. Importantly, you need to take advice from financial and business advisors on whether the franchise is viable, and from attorneys on the legal side of the franchise business.

2.5 Borrowing Money

Funding the initial start-up of your business can be difficult. You have just started your business and you immediately begin incurring debts with cash that you do not have. I remember when we started our law firm all we had was an overdraft and a credit card. We decided that we did not want to borrow a lot of money to start the business (otherwise we would just be paying a lot of our future profits to the bank), so we never touched the overdraft and established an internal line of credit with our own money.

However, depending on the type of business that you are starting, obtaining finance may sometimes be a necessary step to ensure that you can operate your business through the phases of the Business Legal Lifecycle. If you are starting a business that has large upfront capital costs such as a food supply business, a stationery business or a glass supplier, for example, you will need to spend money to buy your products before you start to sell them to your customers.

There are a number of options available to business owners to access funding to pay for the upfront start-up costs of their business, including:

(a) Lending your own funds to the business

(b) Borrowing money from a bank

(c) Borrowing money from friends or family

(d) Debtor finance

(e) Equipment finance

Lending your own funds to the business

Using your own funds to start your business is obviously a risky proposition; however, if you have the cash, it may be your best option. In choosing this option you don't need to worry about how you are going to pay yourself or your debts, and you will be able to generate a realistic projection of those costs against your income. Ideally, you should prepare a cash flow projection, a full year budget and business plan before you start. Again, at this stage, it is imperative that you obtain advice from key consultants such as accountants and financial planners. You may not be aware of all of the costs that are involved in setting up a business, so it is vital that you properly plan your funding arrangements (if you haven't already done so in the Conception phase).

Borrowing from a bank

If you don't have the cash to fund your own start-up costs, then you need to consider other funding alternatives. Borrowing from a bank is one of the most common methods to fund a start-up business. I am certainly not against banks and, indeed, believe that they are an essential player in setting up and funding your business. However, I have seen business owners work hard to build strong relationships with particular bank managers, only for those bank managers to move on and leave the business owners to deal with a new bank manager and rebuild the relationship from scratch. Or, worse still, because the bank has all of their assets tied up, they use this transition to become stricter in their lending conditions as the personal relationship no longer exists.

From the Case Files

This is exactly the situation that confronted one of our clients with large property holdings. The client had a business in investing and developing large commercial and industrial properties. He owned properties that were valued at over $60 million and was in debt to one bank that had funded him for over 20 years for approximately one third of the value of his properties. When he became embroiled in a dispute with his business partner, and despite the fact that the properties had significant equity, the bank stepped in and prevented my client from exercising his control over his assets without any reason other than the fact that there was a dispute and the bank did not want it to affect the value of the properties it held as security. This caused my client to enter into a protracted legal battle that cost both sides close to a million dollars in legal fees.

Another one of our clients is also a property developer with significant equity in a number of properties. The properties range from residential to commercial and industrial and the client had, over a 10-year period, built a strong portfolio of property assets with significant equity and a very good rental return. The client also had a long-standing relationship with his bank and one bank manager in particular. Just before the beginning of the 2008 global financial crisis (GFC), the client entered into a contract to sell one of his properties. Before entering into the contract, the bank manager told him that he could take 50% out of the sale proceeds to fund another project because the bank had sufficient equity in the other properties. At this time the bank manager suddenly left to pursue a different career. The new bank manager told the client that, as a result of the GFC, the bank tightened their lending criteria and changed their mind, taking all of the funds from the sale. The consequence of this was that the client was forced to secure additional funding through the bank at a higher rate and at a significantly higher cost in fees and lost opportunities. In a situation where the client was hoping to free himself from the constraints of the bank, a change of relationship manager and policy meant that he was even more closely controlled by the bank. Had he been able to secure funding from a different bank, the client would have been able to negotiate a much better deal.

Banks love to take guarantees and security over a number of assets (cross-collateralization), especially when you're first starting your business. For example, the bank will commonly require the directors/shareholders/founders to give a personal guarantee and, if you own a house, the bank may ask for security over the house to support the guarantee so that if you default in the repayments, it can sell your home to repay the debt, as really there is no value in selling the struggling business. This represents a considerable risk, especially if you own the house with a spouse or partner because the bank may require a personal guarantee from that person as well.

This should be avoided if possible as, more often than not, your spouse or partner will not be involved in the business and they risk losing their home as a result of the business going bad. If your bank says 'no', keep looking because you will probably be able to find another five banks that will say 'yes'.

In my experience there are two main strategies when borrowing from banks:

(a) Build relationships with a number of banks and play them off against each other to obtain the most favorable terms, although this can still have negative consequences if one of the bank managers leaves.

(b) Engage an experienced and competent mortgage broker who can liaise with different banks and get the best deal on your behalf. Additionally, it is important to also liaise with an accountant and financial planner so that your consultants know what is going on and can give you the best advice.

Borrowing money from friends or family

Borrowing money from family and friends must be seen as the last resort. When borrowing money from a bank, there is always the risk of the bank stepping in and taking control of the business if things turn sour. If you borrow money from someone you know, be prepared that they are likely to want some involvement in your business. You might be shocked to find that you gained a 'de-facto partner' instead of a lender. Of course people never enter into the transaction with any malice, but unfortunately things can and do go wrong, not only damaging the business but also the relationship with the family member or friend. If you decide to borrow money from someone you know, it's imperative that the agreement is properly documented and clear ground rules are established to regulate the lender's role (if any) in the business so that the relationship is well-managed. Both parties need to understand that they are entering into a serious business transaction; to run the business properly rules are necessary and will be strictly enforced.

From the Case Files

I saw this type of relationship turn sour a few years ago when a business owner came to see me as he had lent money to his son-in-law to start a business. The father-in-law was an elderly gentleman who had worked for a salary all his life and he had built up a strong savings portfolio. He wasn't, however, aware of what was required to run a business so when his son-in-law approached him to help with a new business venture, he happily agreed. However, there was no agreement or understanding between them as to what the terms of the lending arrangement were or the level of involvement that the father-in-law had in the business. The father-in-law was concerned that his son-in-law was 'out socializing' instead of working to build the business. He felt that his son-in-law was simply wasting his money and wanted to get his money back. After many discussions he approached his son-in-law accusing him of taking his money and not taking the business seriously. On a positive note, it turned out that the son-in-law had simply been networking and was genuinely trying to build up his business, and that the father-in-law had misunderstood what was going on. Unfortunately, the mistrust caused massive divisions within the family that took years to resolve. Admittedly, this was an extreme case, but it is a real life illustration of how mixing business with family can lead to severe consequences.

On the other hand, I have also seen success stories where this kind of relationship has worked. A client of ours, who had recently retired after 40 years of operating his own business, sought our advice when the person he sold the business to wanted to borrow money from him. The business was a road transport one that had significant overheads in the trucks and machinery used in the business. The new owner had attempted to expand the business into other areas and they had not been successful so he was struggling from an operating cash flow perspective. The new business owner had a house that was virtually unencumbered that they could provide as security for the loan. After many discussions, the client took a commercial stance, engaging independent valuers to value the house and allowing us to properly document the loan.

The documentation clearly set out the rights and obligations of the parties and there was a clear understanding between the old business owner and the new one that the relationship was limited to that of a lender/borrower relationship and the old business owner was to have no involvement in the business.

By dealing with each other professionally and at an arm's length, the transaction proceeded without a hitch and the relationship remains strong.

Borrowing money from family and friends can be risky but with the right advice and proper establishment, it can work.

Debtor finance

Debtor finance, also called 'invoice discounting', 'debt factoring' or 'invoice lending', is where you accept a percentage payment from a bank or debt factoring company on the value of the invoices you have issued to your customers or clients. The debt factoring company then assumes the responsibility to chase payment of the full amount of the invoice and they pocket the difference.

For certain types of businesses that require immediate cash flow to buy stock (e.g. a printing business) this type of finance can be of great assistance, especially in the short-term start-up phase before cash flow is enough to maintain liquidity.

There are a number of issues that can arise with debtor finance:

- You 'lose' a significant amount of your profit
- Usually if the debt is not paid within a set timeframe, for example 60 days, you are required to pay the money back to the debt factoring company that has provided it to you. You do not get any of your interest or other cash back and you lose that money
- Your ability to borrow from other lenders may be affected as your book debts will not be available as security for other borrowing options
- Customers may not like dealing with a third party on the payment of their debts

If you opt to use this type of finance, you should ensure that it is a short-term fix to your operating cash flow problems as it will seriously impact upon your profits. Again, it is imperative that you obtain the right advice from your attorney, accountant, financial planner and/or mortgage broker to ensure that all of your circumstances are considered and that it is the right funding option for you.

Equipment finance

Another common funding avenue for business owners is equipment finance, which is commonly used when a business needs a piece of equipment or a vehicle. There are many different options and you need to ensure that you get the best deal for your business in terms of start-up cash flow and value for money.

Your accountant, financial planner and mortgage broker will assist here in getting you the best deal. Beware of the latest deal from a financier or a vehicle dealer, which will usually result in you paying the full price for the vehicle (or piece of equipment) as well as paying interest on the loan.

From the Case Files

A client of ours had a business that had two different premises. It was an accounting firm that had two owners who visited both offices on a regular basis as they had significant clients at both office locations. The different premises were more than 50 miles apart.

This meant that the business owners needed a number of vehicles to travel between the two business premises. The client used the services of a broker on the basis that the purchase price was being paid upfront. This meant that the client, when negotiating the purchase price of the vehicles, was able to receive the lowest available market price and interest rate for the vehicle. This differs to the situation where you might take finance directly from the vehicle company, who will usually have a competitive interest rate but you will end up paying a higher price for the vehicle.

2.6 Insurance

As a business owner, you or your business may be liable for a variety of damages or injuries that occur on your business premises or through the work that you perform. Insurance is an agreement where an insurer undertakes to provide a guarantee for compensation to an injured or wronged person for certain types of damage suffered by that person. It was introduced to help spread the risk for business owners amongst the community and to ensure that injured persons are paid compensation to help them with their injuries.

There are different types of insurance that you will need for your business. If you have leased premises or a franchise agreement, the formal documents will set out the types of insurance that are required. The most common types of insurance that you need to consider are:

(a) General liability insurance

(b) Professional indemnity

(c) Product liability

(d) Plate glass

(e) Business interruption

(f) Inventory insurance

There are other types of personal insurance that will be discussed in section 8 on Estate Planning.

General liability insurance

General liability insurance allows business owners to protect themselves from general claims for injury caused by negligence. For example, if a member of the public injures themselves on your business premises because they slip on water that is on the ground without a warning sign and that should have been cleaned up, the injured person can make a claim for compensation through this type of insurance for any injury or loss (for instance medical costs) that they suffer.

Professional indemnity insurance

This type of insurance is necessary for businesses providing advice or services within specific industries. These can include where a professional has breached an obligation to provide advice by:

- Providing negligent advice
- Not achieving the result required by a contract
- Giving bad financial advice
- Providing incorrect nutritional advice

Professional indemnity insurance can also cover a business owner against claims involving the provision of services, including:

- Incorrectly auditing a company's accounts
- Inappropriate surgical procedures

While some industries have their own specific insurance that covers professional indemnity, this type of insurance is absolutely necessary for the majority of businesses to ensure that they are protected should their advice be deemed a breach of the law or negligent.

Product liability insurance

If your business sells or produces a product, then you will need to consider product liability insurance. This insurance protects a business owner against a claim if your product causes:

- Injury or death
- Property damage
- Emotional distress or psychiatric illness

The point of this insurance is to protect you if there is a fault or failure in your product so that if you are deemed negligent and liable to pay compensation to someone who purchased your product, then you can continue to operate your business as the insurance pays the compensation.

Plate glass insurance

Where a premises has a glass shopfront or uses a lot of glass, a landlord will invariably require the tenant to insure the glass against damage, whether intentional or accidental. For instance, where the business is part of a shopping mall or a strip of shops, damage may be caused by someone throwing a rock or deliberately damaging the glass in your shop or business premises. This type of insurance ensures that the damage is quickly and easily fixed without a dispute between the landlord and business owner over responsibility for the damage.

Business interruption insurance

Where a business is affected by or is unable to trade due to circumstances outside its control (for example a natural disaster), business interruption insurance covers the loss of income for the period throughout which the business is affected, including the repair times. The actual amount that can be claimed will depend on the type of business and the type of loss suffered. An example of a natural disaster that affects a business is flooding; such an event is not the fault of any party but it can affect the ability of a business to trade from its premises by restricting team and customer access. Policies vary widely between insurers and most have extensive exclusions so business owners need to compare policies carefully to understand how a policy's restrictions may affect a claim and to find the one that offers the best coverage for their particular business.

Inventory insurance

Any business that relies on its inventory, stock and/or products for its income should have inventory insurance to cover it for the replacement of stock and products in the event of a disaster. The purpose of this insurance is to ensure that where the stock or products are damaged through no fault of the business, its employees or the business owner, they can be replaced and the business can continue to trade.

An insurance policy is a contract

When you obtain an insurance policy you are entering into a contract with the insurance company. Before you enter into such a contract you need to obtain competent advice from an insurance broker, an attorney, or both. Any insurance contract will very carefully set out the conditions of insurance and, more importantly, the limitations of that cover, called exclusions. Consult with your attorney in relation to these conditions and exclusions to ensure that you are aware of what exactly your insurance covers and what it does not.

2.7 Conclusion

As we have seen, the considerations that go into the Start-up phase are extensive and require a great deal of advice from a range of different consultants. If all of the matters covered in this section are not considered at this stage, you may find that once you do eventually get around to considering them, you will have incurred additional significant costs because of the delay. A very common example is where a business begins as a sole proprietor, and later it is transitioned into a company, whereby it incurs tax and duty costs for the transfer along with the legal and accountancy costs in doing so.

Similarly, without early advice as to the terms of the lease, you may be two or three years into a five or 10-year lease, and realize that you have agreed to an uncommercial term that will cost you a significant amount of money down the track. As the lease is a binding contract between the business owner and the landlord, it cannot be changed and, if you want to stay in the premises long term, you may have significant issues trying to renegotiate the terms of the lease, even with legal advice.

Evaluating the different aspects of this phase slowly and carefully will ensure that you successfully set up your business on sound financial footing. I have seen many business owners rush their way through this phase and not consider the implications of their actions, incurring them thousands of dollars in unnecessary costs. Once you have successfully navigated your way through Phase 2 – Start-Up, you are ready to proceed into Phase 3 – Initial Clients.

QUESTIONS TO ASK BEFORE YOU PROGRESS TO THE NEXT PHASE:

1. Have you set up the correct structure for your business?
2. If you are entering into a lease, is it on commercial terms that you are happy with?
3. Have you created your brand?
4. Do you have a clear path for funding your business so that you can operate successfully?
5. Do you understand your responsibilities as a business owner?
6. Do you have management experience? If not, where can you turn to get the right advice?

CHAPTER 3

Phase 3 – Initial Clients/Customers

Once you have set up your business properly, it is time to start finding clients to pay your costs, expenses and, of course, yourself. I personally find the Initial Clients phase to be the most interesting and enjoyable of the first three steps of the Business Legal Lifecycle. This is because you are starting to put all of your efforts from the first two phases into practice. However, Phase 3 can also be a daunting time because you are worried as to whether or not your business will be a success, and this is when you start to find out. The good news is that once you get through this phase, the business will start to turn over good revenue and you can concentrate on other aspects of the business as it progresses through the Business Legal Lifecycle. During this phase I will discuss:

- Identifying your ideal client
- Tracking the source of your work
- Choosing whether you should work for only one client or a government body
- Your initial terms of trade or agreement with your clients or customers
- Debt recovery proceedings and processes

Important considerations during this phase are:

- Who is my ideal client? What do they look like? What do they do? Where do they hang out? What magazines do they read? What cars do they drive? Who are their customers?
- How do I market my business to my ideal clients? Do I advertise? Should I use social media? Should I focus on building relationships with partners first? What other options do I have?
- What processes do I have in place to sign up clients?
- What procedures do I need to make sure that my debts are paid?

Dangerous ways of thinking during this phase are:

- Worrying that you are not going to get any clients
- Thinking that you need to accept all of the work that comes your way irrespective of its quality
- Not establishing the right documentation when engaging your customers to ensure that your customers are legally bound to pay your bill
- Not having the appropriate debt recovery measures in place

3.1 Who is your Ideal Client/Customer?

During this phase, you need to identify who the ideal clients or customers are for your business. For example, at our law firm, we determined that we wanted to work with small-to-medium-sized businesses (with a turnover of less than $100 million) and their owners. We also then went through and questioned:

- How old are they?
- How much property do they own?
- Where do they live?
- Where do they dine out?
- What kind of car do they drive?
- What sports/sporting teams do they follow?
- What do they do in their leisure time?
- Do they enjoy overseas holidays?
- How many team members do they employ?
- What customers do they want to work with?

We then drafted a mind map that displayed each method that we were going to use to find our ideal clients and looked at what strategies we could put in place to maintain relationships with those businesses, individuals and referral partners.

This is a critical step as it will help to focus all of your marketing and other work through the subsequent phases of the Business Legal Lifecycle to target your ideal clients and/or customers. Your alternative is a scattergun approach that will not allow you to focus your marketing resources on your ideal client.

I strongly recommend that you do not take on every customer or client that comes through your door. When you are in the Start-Up phase, you naturally want to engage with as many clients and bring in all the work that you can so that you can start to make money. However, this can be a mistake, as we discovered when we started our law firm.

We took on everyone that came through the door, even if the work was outside our comfort zone, just to build our client base as quickly as possible. As a consequence, we did not focus on attracting our ideal clients and we spent far too much time on work outside our knowledge and expertise.

Luckily, we quickly learnt how to cut back on clients. We identified our A-class clients (clients that pay well and give you lots of work), B-class clients (potential A-class clients but who require some work and training on how to conduct themselves in business) and C-class clients (who would never become A-class clients because their attitude to business was so incompatible to ours that we were not able to do business with them as clients).

We stopped working for C-class clients, and made a decision that we would allow B-class clients a set timeframe (in our case a year) to become A-class clients, or they were going to be cut as well.

Once we implemented this strategy, we were able to work more efficiently and effectively. By not dealing with the issues that are inherent in B-class and C-class clients, it allowed us more time to work with our A-class clients.

3.2 Tracking

'What gets measured gets managed' is a cliché but it rings true with any business. You will find it difficult to manage your business unless you track (at a bare minimum) where your clients and customers are coming from, who is paying you the most, and who is giving you the most repeat business.

There are plenty of great tools out there and if you have a business coach or mentor, you can talk to them about giving you a tool or two to assist in tracking the important aspects of your business.

3.3 Businesses Based on one Client or a Government Body

Based on the nature of some businesses, you may start with only one client, or all of your work may come from the government or a government department. If you do go into this type of business, you need to consider that you are still effectively just an employee rather than a business owner, and are at a high risk of losing the business that you put your heart and soul into.

Building a business with only one client or customer is extremely risky as the business is based on one relationship; if that relationship breaks down it could be a severe blow, possibly catastrophic, to your business. Any agreement that you enter into needs to ensure guaranteed levels of work with sufficient notice to find a new source of income if the contract ends. From my experience, this type of business is extremely risky and can place the business owner in severe financial hardship if they fail.

From the Case Files

One of our clients purchased an existing business which only had one customer and worked exclusively for them. The business was a construction business that did repairs for a larger building business to fix defective work. The client's work for this one particular client was on a contract basis but the work was so specialized in conducting repairs for the one particular type of work that the client had no other clients. Due to the nature of the work, there were no other potential customers for the business. The previous owner who sold the business was friendly with the exclusive client. A dispute arose between our client and the previous business owner on a personal level. The business started to suffer financial difficulties, and then the previous owner ensured that the sole client gave the new business owner no more work. They did this simply out of spite, which in effect destroyed the business as it had no other source of work. Eventually the creditors of the business would no longer wait for payment and the company that operated the business was wound up and the buyer had to take a job at another company.

3.4 Where are you Going to get the Clients from?

As previously mentioned, finding clients is a major challenge that all businesses face. This is not something you can put off – you need to know where to find new clients. In our case, the mind mapping exercise proved extremely beneficial in helping us to develop a variety of avenues to obtain new clients and we were able to put these strategies in place.

Avenues for finding new clients include:

- Creating strategic alliances (these are relationships where two businesses work closely together to cross-refer business between themselves) with businesses that already work with your ideal client
- Hosting beneficiary relationships (these are relationships where a business will refer work to your business without the expectation that they will receive cross referrals) with businesses that already work with your ideal client
- Attending regular networking groups
- Fostering repeat business from existing clients
- Contacting referrals from existing clients
- Building an online presence through your website and social media
- Exploring marketing and advertising options

It is up to you to explore these options in greater detail and work out which are right for you. By testing and measuring different options, you will be able to see which ones work best for you and even find new ones you hadn't considered. Make sure that you discuss these different options with your business coach or mentor (if you have one), as there may be other methods that you have yet to consider. You will find that you will be constantly adjusting and testing these throughout your Business Legal Lifecycle.

3.5 Your Initial Agreement/Terms of Trade

I have seen many occasions where a business is established, starts engaging with customers and clients, but does not have properly organized processes in place to engage with their clients. Where this occurs, it can be difficult for you as a business owner to enforce your agreement with the customer and/or client as there will inevitably be a dispute over certain details. A comprehensive agreement or terms of trade allows for a number of important aspects of the business and customer/client relationship to be formally documented and if you have such an agreement in writing that clearly sets out all of the terms and expectations, such disputes can be avoided. Some of the aspects may include (this list is not exhaustive and you should consult with your attorney to develop a comprehensive list of required terms and conditions):

- The scope of the work to be performed
- The timeframe for the work to be performed
- The timeframe for payment
- Resolving disputes between the parties
- Enforcing payments if there is a default by the customer or client
- Warranties and conditions

Often a new business owner will be reluctant to spend valuable time and money drafting a formal agreement in the Initial Clients phase. This is an error that too many new business owners make as they start engaging with customers or clients with either a very short agreement, or nothing at all. Although a great deal of work may be done, enforcing payment of invoices if the relationship sours can be difficult in the absence of a firm agreement. It can also be difficult to change a basic agreement to a more comprehensive agreement at a later date, as the customer/client may be concerned about your motives in making the change and be hesitant to accept a new agreement.

Of course, if you are just starting out, it may be cost prohibitive to engage an attorney or other consultant to draft these types of agreements. However, as soon as you attract a few clients, it is imperative that you draft appropriate terms and conditions for your business. Make sure, though, that the documentation is tailored for your business, and is not simply a pro-forma document without any consideration of the particular requirements of your business and situation.

Beware!

Perhaps the biggest challenge that business owners face is that their agreement does *not* actually define the scope of the work being performed. The scope of the work must be clearly set out so that there can be no confusion or misunderstanding as to what is (or is not) to be completed.

From the Case Files

A client of ours was operating a business that provided custom made products to builders specific to each different building in which they were being installed. As they were custom made items, they could not be used in other construction works as they would not suit. The business operated with one major client and a number of minor clients with the major client being on board from this phase in the Business Legal Lifecycle. Unfortunately, the agreement between the parties was a handshake agreement and a written agreement (although discussed on many different occasions) had never been formalized. A dispute arose between the parties as to the terms of payment for a job that, whilst our client had prepared the item correctly, their major client could no longer use due to a dispute with their end user. The major client alleged it was a term of the agreement that our client would not be paid if the end user did not pay the major client. Our client said that this was never agreed. The dispute lasted a number of months and ultimately ended the working relationship between the parties despite the fact that there had not been any issues during the first three or so years of the business relationship. Due to the fact that the parties had never entered into a formal written agreement, there was no easy mechanism to resolve the dispute nor was there any way for the client to enforce the fact that they had complied with their requirements. The business owner was left with the choice of either commencing proceedings to sue for their loss or walk away. Both options would have left them severely out of pocket. Ultimately, they decided to drop the debt but had they had a proper written agreement in place, this would have been avoided as it would have spelt out all of the terms and conditions for payment which could have then been enforced.

3.6 Debt Recovery

If you provide any form of credit to your customers and/or clients, you will need a debt collection procedure in place to protect the cash flow of your business. I will discuss more about debt collection court proceedings and the process of debt collection in section 10.3. You will have heard that 'cash is king' for any business;

this refers to the operating cash flow of a business. The debts that are paid to your business from your customers and clients are your operating cash flow. It is vital, especially in the early days of your business, that you are paid by your customers and clients as quickly as possible, so that you can pay your debts as and when they arise. Ideally, you should ask clients to pay upfront for your work or at least stage progressive payments as the work proceeds. If you are unable to do that then you should consider making payment due upon completion of work or delivery of your product.

However, if your customers and clients need a little more time, use seven or 14 day accounts. The reason for this is that you will have accounts that will be due and payable at various times, and you must always ensure that your accounts payable do not exceed your debtors so that your business has sufficient operating cash flow available for you to pay off the debts of your business.

3.7 Conclusion

It is never too late to introduce formal processes into any business. Without the proper documentation, your business will face increasingly larger risks through the later phases of the Business Legal Lifecycle. The correct implementation of these procedures are essential for your business as timely payments of your debts will ensure that your business operates profitably and that you have plenty of cash flow.

The various matters discussed in this phase will, if properly implemented, ensure that you do not replicate problems in the future. Just remember that if you think that you are busy in these early phases of the Business Legal Lifecycle, you will find that further down the track you will only get busier and you will continue to put these considerations off. Taking action during this phase will assist you greatly in building your business and will enable you to take on employees in the next phase of the Lifecycle.

QUESTIONS TO ASK BEFORE YOU PROGRESS TO THE NEXT PHASE:

1. Have you determined who your ideal client is?
2. Have you determined how you are going to market your business to your ideal client?
3. Do you have a process to sign up clients and document the agreement properly?
4. Do you have debt collection procedures in place?

CHAPTER 4

Phase 4 – Bringing on Employees

As your business grows, so will the demands on your time forcing you to consider bringing in people to help you. There are many different types of employees that you can engage, but the first one will be the most crucial to get right.

I have seen many businesses learn this lesson the hard way in the early days as they employ team members who, while being enthusiastic and dedicated, are simply not suited to their role. This means that they are forced to find new team members quickly which takes up valuable time and resources.

The dip

In navigating your way through the Bringing on Employees phase of the Business Legal Lifecycle, you will eventually realize that you now have, or will soon have, a business that you can really leverage and take to the next level. You will notice that the Business Legal Lifecycle displays a dip after you start to employ people.

Peaks and troughs are a natural part of running a business; there will be times when everything is going well and you are making great profits, and other times when you will experience a dip. Rather than being frightened of this occurring, you should simply be prepared so that the dip has minimal impact on your business.

Engaging employees probably causes the greatest dip, but it can also provide the greatest rewards. There is a dip because your profits decrease as you are now paying wages. You are also spending your time training team members to work the way that you want them to. Once you learn to leverage your employees, they will become the lifeblood of your business and will be integral to your success.

Important considerations during this phase are:

- Do I have sufficient existing work to engage employees?
- Do I have a sufficient pipeline of new clients to justify engaging employees?
- What exactly do I want my new employees to do?
- Will they be engaged as employees or contractors?

- What will the cost be to the business in terms of remuneration, training, employment costs and compulsory payments?
- What laws do I need to comply with in engaging employees?
- Do I need any new insurances (e.g. workers' compensation)?
- Do I need a third party recruiter to find the right person?
- What must I do in the business to leverage my new employees?

Dangerous ways of thinking during this phase are:

- Nobody can do the work better than me
- An employee will take money out of my pockets
- I cannot trust anyone else to deal with my clients/customers
- What will I do if an employee leaves and takes my clients/customers?
- The business is mine and I am not risking it with anyone else

Types of employees

Different types of roles you may want or need to hire include:

- **Secretary/receptionist** – This person will be your right-hand. Not only is this one of the most important roles in a business but also the most challenging to get right. Whilst not every business will need a secretary/receptionist, where there is one, they are usually the first point of contact, whether it be on the phone or in person, for new and existing clients and customers. First impressions matter and may be the difference between winning and losing a customer or client. How many times have you telephoned a business and spoken to someone who was clearly not interested in their job, or walked into a business where the secretary/receptionist kept their head down and did not greet you in a friendly manner, or worse, did not greet you at all? How did you feel about that business? Your immediate impression was probably negative and may have influenced your decision about whether or not to work with that business. It is important that you employ a secretary/receptionist that actually wants to do the job. Some people see the secretary/receptionist role as an entry point or 'stepping stone' to another role in the business. You need to ensure that prior to hiring a new secretary/receptionist, you talk with the candidates to make sure they understand how vital the role is, how crucial they are to the success of the business, and to speak openly about their expectations and goals in applying for the role.

- **Administration** – whether this is a personal assistant, accounts manager, office manager or an internal book keeper, ensure you hire someone who fits your requirements for your business.
- **Workers/fee earners/sales or service team** – after the secretary/receptionist, these employees are the next most important contact point for customers and clients. These are the people who interact with clients and customers on a daily basis, generate revenue and ultimately help you to build your business. The right worker/fee earner/sales or service team member can greatly assist your business and, equally, the wrong hire has the potential to cause irreparable damage.

During this phase I will discuss the difference between employees and contractors, some tips on the interview process, your agreement with your new team member, considerations of your liability as an employer, and the importance of an employee handbook.

Obligations on employers

When you bring on employees it is crucial that you consider the additional obligations that will be placed on you as an employer. Important considerations that can be missed are not withholding the right amount of tax, not paying the right amount of pension contributions and, if they are contractors, not paying appropriate tax. When bringing on an employee it is very important that you speak to your accountant or book keeper to make sure that you are making proper provisions for these amounts and paying them when they fall due. Not doing so has led to the downfall of many businesses and you need to ensure that you comply with the requirements so that this does not happen to your business.

4.1 Employee vs Contractor

One of the biggest mistakes that business owners make is failing to understand the legal distinction between an employee and a contractor or consultant. In the United States, there are specific rules and criteria that determine whether a person is an employee or a contractor. In certain types of businesses, such as the building and construction industry, individuals may technically be employees but are known as contractors and treated as such. Often contractors are called 1099s while employees are called W-2s. These terms come from the tax forms that you need to use when you employ these different types of team members.

Generally, an employee is someone who specifically works in a business; they earn all, or at least the vast majority, of their income from that particular business. They will be a necessary part of the business and the work they perform generally cannot be sub-contracted or delegated to other people. Employees are usually paid on a regular basis for the work performed and the tools or equipment that they need for their work are supplied by the business owner. Finally, an employee does not generally need their own insurance for the work that is performed, as the business owner should have insurance that covers this.

On the other hand, a contractor or sub-contractor is someone who works for a business owner and who can delegate work to other parties without restriction. They are paid on a per job basis as opposed to ongoing, regular payments. A contractor generally has their own tools and equipment and their own insurance. They work with a great deal of independence from the business owner as they also have the option to work for other businesses rather than exclusively with one.

Legal and accounting advice is imperative at this point as employment law is quite complex and there may be serious repercussions if you get it wrong, especially in relation to employer responsibilities, tax and remuneration. This is discussed further in section 4.4. If you employ someone under the wrong classification, it can end up costing you tens of thousands of dollars in unpaid entitlements and penalties. The rules vary from state to state so you need to get the right advice upfront.

From the Case Files

A classic example comes from the construction sector. The company provided services, in particular plumbers, to a large number of different jobs around the country. Approximately 20 team members were engaged as contractors, but according to the appropriate law they may have been considered to be employees. The team worked only for that company, which had insurance covering all team members and supplied all tools and equipment. When a disgruntled employee left the company, he made a complaint to the relevant government department contending that, as he was technically an employee, the employer should have been withholding his tax and paying money into his pension fund. This was even the case where the team member was paid as a contractor, at a higher rate of pay than an employee incorporating tax and pension payments. Unfortunately, it was deemed that he was in fact an employee. The construction company was forced to pay thousands of dollars in unpaid payments, benefits and penalties. The employer's company was then also forced to pay back all of the other contractors because they were also deemed to be employees rather than contractors. If they had looked for the right advice at the start, they may have been able to prevent this sort of decision from coming about by having the right contracts in place and engaging with the team members properly.

4.2 The Interview

Being prepared for a job interview is as important for you as the business owner as it is for the prospective employee. You need to be ready to ask a variety of different questions that establish whether or not the prospective employee is suitable for your business. This will vary depending on the role and the type of business. Consider exactly the sort of person you want for the role before you start interviewing. If you do not do this, you will find yourself flying blind through the hiring process.

A business owner also needs to be aware of the law in relation to what they can and cannot ask a prospective employee. Most of these are common sense but, if you are unsure, then you should seek advice from your attorney or employment consultant.

4.3 The Agreement with your Employee or Contractor

Whether you hire employees or contractors, it is essential that you have watertight agreements in place so that there is no confusion as to the roles and responsibilities of each party. To ensure your agreements are sufficient to cover you from any wrongdoing by the team member and that the team member is correctly classified, you should engage with your attorney or employment consultant. In some cases, industry bodies can also assist with legal advice for business owners to ensure that they comply with these requirements. These agreements should be done as soon as you engage an employee and should not be left until later as you will have problems implementing the contracts. It is much easier to have an employee sign a contract when they start working for you than to wait until there is a problem in the future.

An employment contract also serves to protect the business owner when an employee or contractor stops working for the business. The protection is twofold: firstly, a restraint of trade will stop the employee from competing with your business in an unreasonable fashion; secondly, a confidentiality agreement will protect your information so that the employee or contractor cannot take that information without your consent or agreement.

Many business owners like to take 'barbecue advice' from friends and other business owners in relation to restrictive covenants/restraint of trade issues. They are advised that restraints of trade are not worth the paper they are written on as they are too difficult to enforce. This is not true; a properly worded restraint of trade that protects the legitimate business interests of the business owner will be enforceable. These are highly technical documents and you need to ensure that when they are drafted, they are done correctly to protect your interests as a business owner.

I have personally seen many business owners fall into the trap of relying upon a handshake agreement with their team instead of a written agreement. An employee leaves, and after a few weeks or months customers or clients start to disappear, only for the business owner to discover that they have gone to the ex-employee's new place of work. With an appropriately drafted agreement, this can be prevented as the written agreement can be used to enforce the restraint of trade through the courts.

4.4 Liability for Employers

As I mentioned previously, one of the distinctions between employees and contractors is the level of liability that the business owner has for the acts or omissions of the team member in doing the work of the business. Where the team member is an employee, the employer is liable for all of the work that the employee does for the business. This is the reason (as mentioned in section 4.1) why an employee does not need their own personal insurance for the work they do. The employer is what is called 'vicariously liable' for the work of the employee.

Depending on the type of work and the method used to engage a contractor, the contractor may be personally liable for the work that they have performed for the business owner. There is a lengthy list of factors that have to be considered in determining this; however, if you are going to engage contractors, you need to carefully consider who is liable for the work performed.

Understanding your liability when hiring team members is critical to successfully navigate your way through this phase. You should consult with your attorney and employment consultant to discuss these requirements and what steps need to be put into place to protect you and your business from liability.

An example of this distinction is in the cleaning industry. You may contract a cleaning company, but the person who does the work does so as an independent contractor engaged by the cleaning company. If that is the case, then the person engaged as an independent contractor is liable for any damage that they cause. If the person is an employee, then the main company is liable for any mistakes or damage caused.

4.5 Employee Handbook

As your team grows, it is important to set rules for their conduct within your business through workplace or office policies, commonly within an employee handbook. This will depend heavily on the type of business that you operate. Some important considerations when drafting the policies include (this list is not exhaustive):

- Dress standards
- Drug and alcohol use
- Workplace harassment (both sexual harassment and bullying)
- Racial, religious and other types of vilification
- Breaks
- Grievance procedures
- Email use
- Internet use
- Social media use

When you create a policy for your business you are setting out instructions, rules and regulations for your business. This will ensure that the team (both employees and contractors) understands the standard of conduct expected of them and their colleagues and the consequences of any breaches. They are also critical to protect you and your business if a problem occurs so that you are able to demonstrate that the appropriate systems were in place to deal with such problems. This can be used as a defense should an employee (or a former employee) make a claim of negligence against you.

There is no 'one size fits all' solution for the policies or an employee handbook. You should consult with an attorney or employment consultant in drafting these policies to ensure that they are tailored to your business's unique requirements.

For a business in the Start-Up or Bringing on Employees phase of the Business Legal Lifecycle, the cost of having these policies drafted and put in place may seem prohibitive. Employee handbooks are often left until a business is well-established and with many employees. However, once you have four or five members on a team (in addition to the business owner or owners), it is extremely important that these policies are in place as you will find it necessary to set the rules and expectations of your team (both employees and contractors) to save you time and money.

This will not only give you comfort that your team members have guidance on important issues, but it will also increase the value of your business as a good system will be of value to a prospective buyer. You must also ensure that the employee handbook is agreed to by your team; this is usually done within their employment contract.

4.6 Conclusion

Richard Branson once said, 'Train employees well enough so that they can leave. Treat them well enough so that they do not want to leave.' This really rings true for me as an employer. When the business is in the Start-Up phase, the business owner is the person that does all of the work, deals with all of the clients and wears all of the hats. As your business grows, you need to be able to relinquish some of that control and employ a team to do that work for you. If you micro-manage your team, they will not develop the confidence and skillset that they need to become a valuable asset to your business.

Additionally, they may feel undervalued, dissatisfied and eventually leave, forcing you to find and train someone new at a considerable loss of time and money. It is natural during this phase of the Business Legal Lifecycle for you to start thinking, 'my team members aren't learning fast enough', 'employing this person was a mistake', or 'I need to take over and do the work myself'. It is important to remember, however, that the vast majority of business owners were once employees or contractors themselves.

So think about what it was like when you started off as an employee or contractor and how you developed into your role over time. This eventually led you to the point where you were trained well enough to stay. Then, think to yourself, 'why did I leave?' If you can put policies and procedures in place to treat your employees and contractors well enough so that they do not want to leave, they will become trusted and valued members of your team.

Once you have properly navigated this phase of the Lifecycle you will know that you have a business that can be leveraged. You will probably experience a dip in your business because you are spending time and money on training the new employee(s) but by properly navigating this phase, you will be able to minimize that dip and be ready for the next phase: Protecting your Intellectual Property and subsequent phases.

QUESTIONS TO ASK BEFORE YOU PROGRESS TO THE NEXT PHASE:

1. Do you want to bring on employees? (If no then move straight onto the next phase.)
2. Are you ready to bring on employees?
3. Do you need a third party recruiter to find the right person?
4. What do you want your new employees to do?
5. Are they employees or contractors?
6. What is the cost of bringing on employees?
7. Do you have to put in place any new insurance (e.g. employer's liability)?

CHAPTER 5
Phase 5 – Protecting Intellectual Property

'Intellectual property' is the legal term given to the assets of a business that have been created by the business owner, their team or consultants in the course of their employment and includes trademarks, literary and artistic works, designs, inventions, trade secrets, customer lists, processes, procedures, know-how, partnership agreements, business names and images and so on. It is imperative that you put steps in place to properly protect your intellectual property or you could risk irreparable damage to your business. If, further down the track you decide to sell (see section 11) or franchise (see section 7) your business, your intellectual property is the asset that will form the base of any potential sale or franchise.

This phase is all about identifying, protecting and setting up structures to ensure that third parties cannot steal your intellectual property. While it may seem that this phase should occur much earlier in the Business Legal Lifecycle, the practical reality is that most start-up businesses do not have the resources to take this step until after they have a viable business and start to leverage their employees. It is for that reason that we have included this phase at this stage of the Business Legal Lifecycle.

In this section I will discuss trademarks, establishing a separate entity to own your intellectual property, licensing your intellectual property, how-to guides and checklists for the work done in your business, and patents.

The Protecting Intellectual Property phase follows straight after the Bringing on Employees phase and is situated on a downward slope of the Business Legal Lifecycle (see image on page 11). As long as the business owner is a sole operator, their intellectual property is safe. Once they engage employees, the need to protect their intellectual property suddenly becomes important. When a business owner first starts out, they will more than likely have all of their ideas and methodology in their head. This intellectual capital is the most important and valuable asset that the business owns.

Once a business brings on employees, the business owner faces the challenge of communicating and explaining their ideas and processes to their employees, usually through documentation and training programs. This information is no longer safe inside the business owner's head, but is shared with others who may, without adequate protection and safeguards in place, use this information for their own benefit rather than for the business.

Important considerations during this phase are:

- What is my brand?
- How am I going to protect the brand?
- Is my brand unique enough to protect?
- Will anyone else want to buy my brand?
- How do I protect my intellectual property?
- What other intellectual property do I need to protect?
- If I was to buy my business, what intellectual property would I need to own and what would convince me to pay more for the business?
- How do I teach my team what I know about my business?

Dangerous considerations during this phase are:

- I do not have time to consider protecting my intellectual property
- Nothing will ever happen to my intellectual property anyway so why bother?
- No one will want my brand
- No one can do what I can do, no matter what systems I put in place

5.1 Trademarks

What is a trademark?

A trademark is essentially your unique name, logo or symbol that the outside world uses to recognize and acknowledge your business or product. Generally speaking, if you have a unique trademark, another person cannot directly or substantially copy that trademark or use it in competition against you. Here, the term 'passing off' applies, as the other business is 'passing off' their business as being the same as or somehow related to or affiliated with your business. If a business is passing off by using a trademark that is similar to yours, for example, you may be able to stop them through the courts. You will need to engage the services of an attorney experienced in these areas to determine what, if any, rights you have in this regard.

Formal registration

Most countries have laws that allow for the registration of trademarks with a government body and, in the US, that's the United States Patent and Trademark Office (USPTO). Each state also has its own registration requirements, so you will need to check these with your attorney. Registration gives formal recognition to the trademark and grants you certain rights and responsibilities in relation to the trademark to replicate in your business. To protect your trademark in the United States, you need to register your trademark in at least one of the 45 categories or classes of goods and/or services. Depending on your business or product, you may need to protect your trademark in multiple classes as a registered trademark only gives you protection rights for the particular class that you are registered in. A registered trademark will generally grant its owner the exclusive and protected use of the trademark from the date that the application for registration of the trademark was made with the appropriate government body such as the USPTO. There is a specific process that needs to be followed so you will likely need the advice of a specialist attorney or patent attorney.

Once you have submitted your application to the USPTO, your proposed trademark will be examined to determine whether it is unique enough to be considered for registration. Considerations include other similar trademarks (whether registered or not) and the likelihood of confusion between your mark and a mark belonging to another business. In the United States, the trademark will either be approved or you will need to make changes to the mark and/or further submissions as to why your trademark should be approved. Once approved, the trademark must then be advertised to see if any third party has any objections to the trademark being granted to you. Once this process is finalized, you are then granted the registered trademark, usually for a period of 10 years.

From the Case Files

We encountered a business owner who did not register their trademark until it was too late. The business was a bakery that had been trading with the same name for 25 years. They had built the business to include 20 stores and they never had an issue with the use of their name. When the business owner decided that he wanted to start franchising the business (discussed in section 7), we discovered that there were a number of other trademarks already registered that competed with his own trademark, and he was unable to use the name of his store/product in the franchise which he could have contested had his trademark been registered. This meant that the business owner had to change the trademark of their business in order to franchise.

International trademarks

If you want to take your business internationally, you will need to first register your trademark in the United States. Once this is done, you can apply to register your trademark globally using the Madrid System through the World Intellectual Property Organization (WIPO). There are over 90 member countries of the WIPO in which protection will be offered to your trademark so long as it does not conflict with another registered trademark in that country. This can be a costly process, as you need to pay application fees to each country. So you need to be clear as to in which countries you intend to trade before you go through this process.

Your protection starts from when you first apply for registration, therefore the earlier that you apply to register a trademark, the better it will be for your business. You will avoid issues that might arise in the future with competing businesses that may mean that you will need to fight for the registration of your trademark. Worse still, you could build a great, sustainable business that is ready to really leverage, only to find out that you have to change the name of your business and lose the vast majority of the goodwill that you have established over the years of trading.

5.2 Separate Entity to Hold your Intellectual Property

In certain businesses you might require your trademark to be held/owned by a separate entity such as a company and which is different and separate from the entity that operates your business. You would do this so that if something goes wrong with the entity running the business, the intellectual property relating to that business is still protected. In my experience, most business owners, when first setting up their business, do not consider the protection they will need if the business fails and this lack of consideration can end up costing them dearly.

Ideally this step should be taken earlier in the Business Legal Lifecycle, preferably during the Start-Up phase. The financial burden to set up separate entities to own different assets can be prohibitive at that stage, so it has been included as part of the Protecting Intellectual Property phase. You need to be aware that if you need a separate entity to hold your intellectual property and have not done so by this phase, there is little point in doing so down the track as the costs and consequences make it uncommercial.

As always, it is crucial that before you take any step in setting up a separate entity you obtain advice from your attorney, accountant, business mentor and other consultants to consider how to structure it correctly for your business.

From the Case Files

An example where a client undertook this change occurred recently. The client was a business that provided professional services as a consultant for third party businesses in relation to issues with their employees. The business had been built from the ground up and had established significant intellectual property that whilst not worth much at the time would be worth more in the future. In the early phases of their business, the owners thought that the idea of separate structures to own their intellectual property was cost prohibitive. As they built their business and developed significant intellectual property and even a book, the client had put all of that at risk with it being owned by the vehicle that traded their business. Being a professional services business, even with insurance, the entity that owned the intellectual property was open to attack if someone wanted to allege that their advice was wrong or negligent. We were able to change the structure at a minimal cost for the clients as the intellectual property had not yet reached its full potential value. This meant that we were able to protect the client's intellectual property in a cost effective manner.

Licensing arrangements

Where you set up the separate entity, you also need to consider what arrangements are put in place to license the use of the intellectual property owned by the separate entity to the trading company. Where you have set up a separate entity to hold your intellectual property or have built a strong intellectual property product (and the franchise model is not appropriate for you – see section 7), you should consider what licensing arrangements you need to have in place as without a license agreement the arrangement might be seen as a sham.

Where a separate entity has been set up for this purpose, it is necessary to have an intellectual property license agreement between the entity and the business. This is an agreement that covers a variety of different matters, including: payment of license fees (this can be a great way to distribute profits amongst entities from a tax planning point of view); what happens when the agreement ends (so that if a trading entity fails, the intellectual property is protected); and what happens if there is a dispute with a third party over the intellectual property.

If you decide to license third parties to use your intellectual property, you will have to ensure that you have a variety of clauses additional to those mentioned above. These clauses may include:

(a) The protection of the intellectual property from misuse by the third party

(b) Confidentiality in relation to any aspect of the intellectual property

(c) Ownership over any improvements to the intellectual property generated by the third party

All of these considerations are important but you must ensure that you obtain advice from your attorney and accountant to ensure that the arrangements that are put in place are correct for your circumstances.

<u>From the Case Files</u>

An example of this type of arrangement comes from an education company. The company provided educational material to schools and other educational institutions on indigenous culture including teaching methodology and a curriculum on teaching this topic. The client set up one entity to own the intellectual property of the business and another to trade the business. This meant that the intellectual property was protected in the asset holding company and allowed for the payment of royalties from the trading company to the intellectual property holding company. This type of structure is used commonly where you have a high risk business with valuable intellectual property.

5.3 How-to Guides (including Operating or Process Manuals)

As business owners concentrate on building their business, they get so focused on *doing the job* that they never actually document *how to do the job.* As a business owner, you may be great at doing the job, but how do you educate your employees, franchisees or people that may buy your business in the future on *how* to do your job? The best way to compile all of this information is through checklists, how-to guides, and operating and process manuals.

When we started our business, we found that we were so busy trying to attract and service clients that we had neither the time nor the motivation to document the processes and procedures on the different aspects of our business. Once we started employing a team to handle files and deal with clients directly, we needed to have processes in place that set out our expectations and requirements as to how team members were expected to do those jobs correctly to ensure efficiency and consistency of service to our clients.

While it would seem that beginning this process in the Start-Up phase would be a good idea, we found instead that getting the newly-employed team members to draft the manuals, checklists, how-to guides and other manuals was actually a better way. Why? Everyone thinks differently and we all have different ways to process information.

As a business owner, you want your team members to use and re-use these guides. You want the intellectual property for your business to be clear, concise, and easy to use. By explaining and educating your team on what and how you want things done and getting them to draft the guides that they will use themselves, you are ensuring the documentation will be written in language that is easily understood by the users themselves.

The exact layout of a how-to guide is a decision that you will need to develop in your business with your team. When we first started, we drafted graphic flow charts that set out all of the steps that had to be taken. However, what we found was that our team did not like that format and wanted step-by-step guides, like checklists with explanations on what had to occur at each step. If we did not do this, the team simply would not use the how-to guides and there was no point in developing them.

You do not need an attorney to help you draft these documents, but you should consult with a business mentor or coach – if you have one – as to the different methods and tools you can utilize to build this intellectual property.

5.4 Patents

A patent is a specific legal right conferred on a business owner to protect an invention that they have developed from misuse by third parties. A patent is granted for any device, substance, method or process that is new, inventive and useful. It grants you, as the owner of the patent, the right to exploit the patented idea for at least 20 years in the United States.

The invention needs to be dissected into its various parts and steps and documented accurately to ensure that the invention is properly protected. Patents are complex to draft and require the advice of specialist attorneys or patent attorneys.

If you develop an invention that you believe is unique, inventive and useful, you should seek the advice of a patent attorney to ascertain if the invention is worth protecting before proceeding further.

5.5 Conclusion

As your business grows, you are constantly developing intellectual property. Every business does this, even when they do not know that they are doing it. Your intellectual property may be the key asset of your business, which will become even more apparent if you decide to dispose of the business in the future. It is your unique intellectual property that sets your business apart from your competitors and defines it in the marketplace.

Protecting intellectual property is therefore crucial for any business and, whilst imitation might be the sincerest form of flattery, it is vital that you take the appropriate steps to protect your intellectual property for the future.

By identifying and protecting your intellectual property you are putting the foundations of a successful and profitable business in place. Done properly, it means that your business is ready for the next phase, Maximizing your Business/ Bringing in Investors.

QUESTIONS TO ASK BEFORE YOU PROGRESS TO THE NEXT PHASE:

1. Have you taken the appropriate steps to protect your business's brand?
2. Have you registered your trademark?
3. Have you protected all of the intellectual property?
4. Is your intellectual property now in a position where a third party would want to buy or use it?

CHAPTER 6

Phase 6 – Maximizing your Business/ Bringing in Investors

Once you have established your business properly, have an extensive client base, have hired employees (and/or engaged consultants/freelancers) and protected your intellectual property, you have a proper business asset. A business asset is a business that has the right foundations in place to expand or be sold.

Now that you have built a proper business asset, your next step is to consolidate your business to maximize the business and team that you have into a well-oiled machine. By consolidating at this point, you will avoid the pitfalls that are commonly encountered as you move into the next phase of the Business Legal Lifecycle.

The Maximizing your Business/Bringing in Investors phase (Maximizing phase) covers maximizing your business through your existing channels, fully utilizing your team and/or attracting investors. As a business owner, you will have the choice between these options (or even doing all of them) but if you have not guided your business properly through all of the preceding phases of the Business Legal Lifecycle, any inherent problems or incomplete systems will be amplified during this process.

The Maximizing phase is the time when you review your business, identify your strengths and weaknesses, and decide how you will consolidate your business. This step involves investing a lot of time and energy into the business to ensure that all of the previous phases are finalized so you can move into the larger growth phases of the Business Legal Lifecycle.

Inviting investors into a business is not a step that will work for every business or business owner. When an investor enters, you lose a portion of control, income and capital in your business. Many business owners I have advised over the years have not wanted to relinquish control and consequently never brought in investors. These owners built their business themselves and wanted to maintain control and continue to work in the business.

As a business owner, it is important that you know what you want before you go further. Just because you have been advised that it is a good idea to bring in an investor, if you are not ready or eager to take this step, it could have disastrous consequences. For example, an investor who wants too much day-to-day input into your business may not be a good fit as an active participant in your business if they lack the necessary knowledge or expertise.

This phase is at the bottom of the dip in the Business Legal Lifecycle (see image on page 11) for the simple reason that if a business successfully navigates this phase, it will be set for growth and prosperity in the future. In this chapter, I will discuss the different options, key documents and considerations that you need to think about during and after this phase. It is important to note that this phase does not include expanding the business, franchising or licensing your business (see section 7).

Important considerations during this phase are:

- What can I invest in for my business that will maximize my returns?
- What work could I be doing right now that I have not yet done?
- How can I get more work?
- Do my existing systems and procedures allow me to scale my business without amplifying problems and issues?
- Is there another market that my business can expand into and what are the benefits of expanding?
- What control over my business/company will I give up if I accept investor money?
- Am I happy to give up some of the income or control over my business in return for investor money?
- How well do I know the investor, their business goals and their alignment with my goals and ideals?

Dangerous considerations during this phase are:

- I do not need to consolidate; I know what I am doing
- I do not want to lose control of my business
- I should take this step as everyone tells me that I should do it
- I cannot trust anyone else with my business

6.1 Maximizing your Business

Before you start to maximize your business, you need to ensure that you have properly navigated your way through the earlier phases of the Business Legal Lifecycle. If you skipped or rushed through the earlier phases, you will not be able to successfully navigate this and subsequent phases. During this phase you need to revisit the previous phases to confirm that you have everything set up correctly; for example, ensuring that the:

(a) Business structure is established correctly

(b) Methods and procedures for engaging with clients are set up correctly

(c) Businesses employees are properly engaged

(d) Intellectual property is properly and sufficiently protected

Once you have these aspects of your business properly established, then you need to seek out new work for your business. Repeat business from existing clients or referrals from existing clients are great methods to build your business but you should also check that you have maximized your team's output to ensure that you are sufficiently protected. Doing this will mean that you have maximized the money that you can make out of your existing employees.

6.2 What to look out for in an Investor

When you accept an investor injecting money or expertise into your business, you usually surrender some control of your business in return for the investment. Depending on how your business is structured and the terms of the investment, the investor becomes a co-owner of your now joint business.

Even if the funds are in the form of a loan and the investor does not take any actual ownership, the investor may still feel they have certain rights or entitlements to the business.

In section 2.5 I discussed some of the perils of taking out loans when third parties invest in a business. The same principle applies here. My experience in this area has shown time and time again that this phase only fails when the owner and investor do not clearly establish from the outset what role the investor will play in the business, the expectations and the return on their investment. There are a number of different legal mechanisms you can utilize to carefully introduce an investor into your business.

These include:

- Selling a share or a percentage of the business to the investor. This usually involves the sale or issuing of new shares in the company. It is important to consider the amount of the investment from both sides of the transaction. Usually, if you operate your business through a company structure, the person having the majority of the ownership will have control over the business. For instance, most day-to-day decisions of a company can be made by those that have a 50% interest, plus one of the voting rights in the entity that owns the business.

  Some bigger decisions may require a bigger percentage; say 75%, plus one of the voting rights in the entity. Whilst it may seem trivial, when a business owner is bringing in an investor, you need to consider the implications of that investment, what the investor gains for their investment, and what the business owner loses.

- Directorship in the company. As discussed in section 2.1, the directors of a company control the day-to-day running of the company. Bringing in an investor as a director will often give the investor a lot of control over the business. Ideally this option should only be considered where the investor makes a large investment and intends to work in the business; otherwise, the investor will have too much control without the business receiving a corresponding benefit.

- Bringing a partner into an un-incorporated partnership or joint venture. In these cases, the new investor assumes an immediate and significant degree of control in the entity, which is a big disadvantage for these types of entities. One implication that can't be overlooked is the need for the dissolution of the old partnership or joint venture, which can have significant tax consequences in certain circumstances.

- Seeking third party loans to assist with expansion. This is a common strategy for businesses such as property development, where an investor may lend funds at a certain interest rate for a limited period of time to allow for the property to be completed. As discussed in section 2.5, both parties need to give careful consideration to the business's capacity to repay the loan.

- Where you seek to bring in an investor, the unique structure of your business will require careful consideration of both the business owner and the investor's point of view to ensure that all parties are satisfied with the outcome. A clear understanding at the beginning of this phase will enable you and the other owners to successfully navigate your way through the further phases of the Business Legal Lifecycle to ensure that you build a strong and profitable business.

From the Case Files

We have worked on many examples of where this approach has worked, one being a client who operated a computer sales and service business. The business was a successful one, turning over around $2 million a year in revenue. The owner decided that he wanted to take the business to the next level and try to reach $5 million in turnover. He knew, however, that he could not fund this himself and that he needed to bring in an investor to inject capital into his business. He had to increase his capacity and find bigger premises; considerations that he could not do on his own.

Whilst trying to decide what to do, the business owner was approached by an investor who wanted to work in his business. The investor negotiated that in return for injecting a large sum of money into the business, he would take a portion of the equity and work in the business with the owner, effectively making them business partners. Both parties followed the process closely and they were able to successfully bring the investor into the business which now trades with a turnover in excess of $5 million with both the original owner and the investor making a significant profit every year.

There are other examples where the process was not followed, and the investor's relationship was doomed to fail. One example was a hairdressing business which was looking to expand. A hairdressing business requires a great deal of investment at start-up – it needs capital to buy the build out, equipment and devices needed to operate the hairdressing business. The business owner was looking for an investor who did not want any hands-on control of the business but simply wanted to take a stake in the ownership of the business.

A suitable investor was found but the parties neglected to document any of the agreements, in particular their expectations and roles. Neither party realized that their understanding of the agreement was totally different. When a dispute arose, as no agreement was in writing, they were not able to resolve the dispute, the relationship broke down and the business had to cease operating. All of this could have been avoided at the outset, had the parties properly documented their agreement.

6.3 Shareholders' Agreements

As previously discussed, the most common structure used to operate a business is a company. One of the main benefits of this structure is that it allows for the easy sale of a percentage of the company to third parties via a documented agreement between the parties. The reason for this is that when a business owner starts a business or brings in an investor, they are usually looking at the world through rose-tinted glasses. However, as in any aspect of life, you need to consider what will happen if things go wrong. Every person in the world has a different personality, things in their lives change, so you need to consider what will happen if that occurs to ensure the continued operation of your business.

A shareholders' agreement is a crucial document that needs to be carefully considered during this phase of the Business Legal Lifecycle. Properly drafted, the agreement will set out the expectations of the parties, the rights and responsibilities of each of the parties, and what happens at the end of the business venture or if there is a dispute. You do not legally require a shareholders' agreement (it is a private contract between the corporation's/company's members), but generally matters considered in a shareholders' agreement are matters that are not necessarily dealt with by a company's articles, such as (this is not an exhaustive list):

(a) The objectives of the business

(b) Confidentiality obligations

(c) Restrictions and procedures on the dilution of a member's interest in the company and/or trust

(d) Capitalization and funding

(e) Dispute resolution mechanisms

(f) Board composition and management arrangements

(g) Procedures for directors' meetings

(h) Policies for dividends

(i) Exit strategies, either for the sale of shares, succession planning or listing the company

(j) Finance policies and what happens if the financial requirements of the entity cannot be funded

(k) Operational procedures

(l) Obligations and rights of members

(m) How loans from shareholders are dealt with by the business

(n) Termination of key people including restraint of trade

(o) Shareholder warranties to each other

(p) Voting rights in relation to specific issues

As stated above, some points may not be applicable to certain businesses and owners. The purpose of this list, however, is to emphasize that drafting this type of agreement requires a great deal of care, consideration and professional advice. A properly drafted agreement will set out the rights and obligations of all parties concerned.

<u>From the Case Files</u>

An example where such an agreement was used was for an accounting practice which had been in operation for over 10 years with a sole owner. The owner had built the business into a well-oiled machine with a number of employees, one of whom decided that they wanted to buy into the business and the original business owner saw this as a good succession plan. The parties engaged our firm to draft a comprehensive shareholders' agreement that set out a very clear and concise process for the parties to run the business and a procedure for when the business was to cease. In the event where there is a dispute between the parties then they have a clear exit path and whilst the business continues to operate, the business partners have a clear understanding of what they are doing and where they are going. Had a proper agreement not been in place they could not have had this reassurance that in the event of a dispute, they are protected.

6.4 Joint Venture Agreements

The term 'joint venture' is commonly used, in a small business context, when at least two parties enter into a partnership but do not want to incorporate a separate structure, such as a corporation/company. Given the nature of a joint venture and its close relationship to a company structure, many of the considerations that I discussed above in section 6.3 apply to a joint venture type of agreement, the most important features being:

(a) The purpose of the joint venture

(b) The responsibilities of the parties in relation to payment of costs and capital payments

(c) Where and how the profits and losses are distributed between the parties

(d) Risk sharing and liabilities

(e) The responsibilities of each of the joint venture parties

(f) The principal place of business of the joint venture

(g) Accounting, records and the bank account for the joint venture

(h) The establishment of an operating committee (who act like directors) for the joint venture

(i) Dispute resolution and assignment of interests in the joint venture

From the Case Files

I have seen many cases where proper consideration was not given to these documents to the detriment of all of the parties to the joint venture's investment. One such example is of a property developer who decided to enter into a joint venture with a third party with whom they had never done any work previously. The joint venture was for the purchase of land, to then obtain development approval on that land to construct a 30 story building, and then to sell the property on to a third party as they had no experience in building that type of construction. We were approached by one of the joint venture parties after it became apparent that the other joint venture party had decided that they no longer wanted to sell the property but wanted to construct the 30 story building. This was despite the fact that neither of the joint venturers had put up any capital, neither had any significant equity in their properties, and neither had ever constructed anything more than a house previously. As there was no agreement in writing though, a dispute arose over what the intentions of the parties, and there was no mechanism to easily resolve a dispute. Therefore, the parties engaged in protracted litigation and lost tens of thousands of dollars in attempting to resolve their dispute. Had they simply discussed the outcome and direction at the beginning of their joint venture, this would not have occurred, and a clear path would have been set. It is also likely that they would not have entered the relationship to begin with as they clearly had different ideas of the ultimate outcome of the project.

Obtaining advice in relation to this type of agreement is also crucial. Getting the right advice from your attorney, accountant and other business advisors will mean that you save yourself a lot of problems and costs in the future.

6.5 Conclusion

Before you set up a structure and draft documentation for third party investment you need to have your business processes and procedures in place to ensure you successfully navigate your way through this phase. You are also acknowledging the strength of what you have put in place for the future of your business.

QUESTIONS TO ASK BEFORE YOU PROGRESS TO THE NEXT PHASE:

1. How can you invest in an aspect of your business to maximize your returns?
2. Do you have sufficient systems and procedures in place?
3. Have you identified another market for your business?
4. Have you properly documented any agreement with an investor in your business?

CHAPTER 7

Phase 7 – Expansion/Franchising/ Licensing or Buying an Existing Business

The expansion, franchising or licensing phase of the Business Legal Lifecycle (Expansion phase) focuses on building your business to be a bigger asset. When a business expands, all of its issues and problems are amplified so, for this reason, this phase closely follows the Maximizing phase of the Business Legal Lifecycle.

The Expansion phase covers the fundamental requirements of expanding your business, including securing new premises or offices, as well as franchising and licensing the business. It is at this point that all your hard work in the preceding phases will begin paying off or, if you skated past some of the fundamentals, the flaws in your business model will be exposed and amplified.

One option that may be open to you to expand your business is to purchase an existing business after giving careful consideration as to the value of the assets you are purchasing, the role they will play in your expansion plans, and how the new business will integrate with your existing business.

From the Case Files

I have seen many businesses try to expand to the point where they simply disperse their problems from one location to many. One accounting firm that we work with started off in just one location, before quickly realizing that they needed a second office closer to the main regional city.

The accounting firm did not properly establish all of their systems and did not put all of the procedures in place. As a result, when they opened the second office, these problems were amplified. For example, their phone and computer systems could not cope with the new requirements of having dual office locations. The firm was forced to quickly put the new systems in place and do twice the work that should have been required.

If these considerations had been dealt with before the expansion of the offices, the problems could have been avoided and the business would not have suffered as a result.

Franchising is not for every business or business owner. When you sell a franchise (see section 7.2) you are selling your business as a product for someone else to use. The business needs to have all of its systems and procedures established correctly before franchising as otherwise you will not be selling the system in its entirety and no one will buy your franchised business.

This phase is positioned in the Business Legal Lifecycle just after the dip caused by the previous phases, because when a business successfully navigates this phase, it is set up for growth and prosperity in the future. I will discuss the different options open to a business at this phase and some of the key documents and considerations that you need to think about to prepare yourself for the next phase.

Important considerations during this phase are:

- Are all of my systems, processes and procedures in place so that I am not going run into problems when I expand, franchise or license?
- Are there other markets my business can expand into, and what are the benefits of expanding my business and brand?
- Do I have a product that other business owners want to use?
- Do I need to bring in a specialist to manage the expansion?

Dangerous considerations during this phase are:

- I can fix all of my problems later
- It does not matter that I do not have my systems in place as the people that buy into my system will just figure it out anyway
- I do not have a brand to protect during the expansion/licensing/ franchising phase of my business
- I do not want to lose control of my business
- I should do this because everyone tells me that I should

- I will work between the multiple business premises and control everything that goes on at all of them without a management structure
- I cannot trust anyone else with my business

7.1 New Business Premises Considerations

Before you secure new business premises, it is important to consider the reasons for this decision and the benefits it will deliver to your business. It is also important to consider what systems and processes you have in place, and how this will be transported to the new premises. If you have a retail shop, for example, you may need to consider things such as the brand of your business, the brand strength (this should have been protected in section 5), your point of sale and ordering systems, as well as the integration between the different premises. Success leaves clues: if you have a successful retail shop in one premises, that design and layout should be replicated so that any returning customer or client recognizes your brand and will respond in a positive manner.

Where your business plans to expand to a second office, it is vitally important to consider how the offices will interact. For instance, careful consideration needs to be given to telephone systems, email and business/practice management software needs. Due consideration must be given to new and emerging technology and how the expansion provides the opportunity to upgrade systems (e.g. internet-based telephones) and processes and increased integration between offices (e.g. Cloud software) for a competitive advantage.

You also need to carefully consider the additional overheads of running another premises. As a general rule of thumb, you should double all your current business costs to cover the costs of the new premises, as it is likely you will have to pay similar rent, outgoings, team costs and so on. You will need to cover the expansion costs from your original business premises until the new business generates sufficient income to support itself and then generate a profit.

It is critically important that you track the performance of your new business premises and monitor the performance between the different premises. These types of processes were discussed in section 3.2 and become even more critically important when you expand your business. Where a business expands, the same considerations in relation to the leasing premises that were discussed in section 2.2 should be revisited. No matter what premises you are looking at for your business, those considerations are crucial.

7.2 Franchise

What is a franchise?

In a franchise, the owner of a business's trademarks, styles, processes, products and systems (franchisor) sells the right to another entity to operate a business using those same products or services (franchisee). In the United States, a franchise structure is one of the most recognizable business structures and is often used by business owners to assist in the expansion of their brand and business. Some states, such as California, have specific laws that relate to franchises. If you want to set up a franchise you need to seek the advice of a local attorney.

A franchise model can be rewarding for both the franchisor and franchisee as a properly established and operated franchise model will allow for a fair amount of control by the franchisor as well as education and support for the franchisee. If you want to start franchising your model, serious consideration needs to be given to the systems that are in place before you sell franchises to other business owners.

When consulted by a prospective franchisor as to how best franchise their business, I advise them to put themselves in the shoes of a franchisee who knows nothing about their business.

The business owner needs to give serious consideration to the knowledge and ongoing support they will need to start and successfully operate a new business. By going through this process, you will readily identify all of the information your franchisee will need to start the business from scratch. Important considerations include (this list is not exhaustive):

(a) Identifying the intellectual property of the business

(b) How the shop and/or shopfront (or other customer-facing space, e.g. restaurant) should be laid out

(c) Employee appearance and presentation

(d) Business operations and documentation of processes and procedures (e.g. the franchise manual)

(e) What agreements does the business have in place with its customers and/or clients?

(f) Employment conditions, including awards

(g) Advertising and marketing campaigns and division of costs between the franchisor and franchisee

(h) Purchase of stock and inventory from preferred suppliers by the franchisee

There are many other considerations that are specific to a particular type of business intended for franchising, thus it is important to ensure that a business is set up correctly and all of the necessary checks and balances are in place before it is franchised.

What are you looking for?

The relationship of franchisor and franchisee is a vital consideration that may be the difference between the success or failure of the franchise. The decision of who to bring into a franchise is like any other business decision; the right one can result in a long and fruitful relationship. However, choosing the wrong franchisee can result in disaster, as you will be stuck in a business relationship that will not work and can lead to the failure of the franchise.

From the Case Files

One such disastrous example is related to an owner of a franchise business that sells coffee and coffee-related products. This franchise company has in excess of 60 franchises and ran a very successful program to bring new franchisees into their business. However, the problem with their business model was that they accepted anyone who applied to be a franchisee of the business meaning they had no control over who came into the business and they had a lot of franchisees who simply were not up to the task. The franchise business had certain procedures in place that required the franchisee to work hard and in particular had a system to achieve a guaranteed goal of cups of coffee sales in any one day. However, as a result of their non-discreet nature of accepting franchisees, one in particular was just not the right fit which resulted in the franchisor unsuccessfully spending a lot of time, money and energy trying to improve the franchisee. This resulted in the franchisee suing the franchisor for alleging that they were not trained properly and both parties lost a lot of money in legal fees.

A more successful example of where a business owner was selective in who they accepted as a franchisee was a pizza restaurant business. The franchisor was a larger company that also owned the franchises of many other different brands in the food and beverage industry. They knew that they had to be very careful and conduct rigorous checks on each prospective franchisee to ensure that they had the requisite business knowledge, they were put through the appropriate level of training, and their financial position had to be sound. Only once a franchisee had passed the checks could they become a franchisee of the business. The franchisor found that they rarely had any issues with the franchisees and, if they did, it was usually due to some other intervening cause.

7.3 Licensing

In some cases, setting up a franchise system may be impractical or cost prohibitive. In such circumstances, you need to consider licensing certain aspects of your business's intellectual property to third parties. Essentially, a license gives the third party the right to use your intellectual property usually in return for a fee. Unlike a franchise, the level of control that is exercised by the licensor is far less as they cannot dictate how the business is owned and operated. The business relationship usually just allows the third party to use the name of the licensor's business to trade with whilst protecting other aspects of the business.

A word of warning here: a business should not use a licensing system in an attempt to get around the complicated requirements for a franchise. Many countries have strict legislation regulating franchising and courts will look to construe an arrangement narrowly as a franchise agreement where there is a dispute and penalize the purported licensor for trying to get around the franchise requirements. The quality of the drafted documentation will be crucial in how a court will determine the matter, so specific expertise will be required to guide you through this legal minefield.

7.4 Buying an Existing Business

Some business owners look to expand their operations quickly by buying an existing business that is owned and operated by third parties. There are a number of advantages and disadvantages to this approach and careful evaluation must be given as to the value and quality of the assets you are buying.

Advantages of buying an existing business include:

- You immediately gain an existing client base
- You can leverage off the existing brand
- The purchase price (which may be high) is offset by an existing income stream
- The new business's processes and systems can be integrated into your business

Disadvantages of buying an existing business include:

- The business may be identified too closely with the previous owner and you may lose a significant number of customers or clients who do not like the change
- You inherit pre-existing issues and problems affecting the business in terms of its systems and procedures
- Careful (and expensive) due diligence will be needed to properly value the business and its assets

Buying the business vs buying the entity

There are two ways that you can buy a business: either you buy the business's goodwill separate from the entity that owns the business, or you can buy the other assets of the business or the entity that owns the business.

A great deal of care needs to be given to purchasing the entity that operates a business as distinct from the business itself. When you buy the entity that operates the business, you are buying all of the history – and potentially all of the problems – of that entity. For example, if the entity owes taxes and you buy the entity, you will inherit that tax burden. When you simply buy the business, you probably won't inherit those issues as they are usually attached to the entity that operated the business in the past.

Before you buy a business, you need to carry out a great deal of due diligence to ensure that you are fully informed about the purchase. This is particularly true if you're also buying the entity that operates the business. A thorough examination of the history of both the business and the entity – with the help of your attorney and accountant – is needed to ensure that all of your concerns are addressed. You also need to consult closely with your accountant to ensure that the books and records of the business or entity are accurate and up-to-date.

7.5 Conclusion

Setting up your business properly will help to increase your revenue and business profile exponentially. If you get this phase wrong, however, it can cost you thousands in extra fees, taxes and potential penalties down the road. Your decision as to whether you decide to simply expand to new premises, buy an existing business, franchise or license your product, will be influenced by your lifestyle goals, expectations and maturity of your business. To get through the Expansion phase, you will need detailed and specific advice from your accountants, attorneys, financial planners and other consultants, to ensure that the decisions you make fit in with your goals and plans for the future.

The decisions that you make for your business during this phase and the advice that you take will determine whether you can take your business to the next level. I have seen too many clients and business owners take short cuts during this phase, whether to reduce costs or to simply save time, with disastrous results that could have easily been avoided. By carrying out your due diligence, taking advice and making measured, considered decisions, you will find that you have a successful business and are ready to move on to the next phase of the Lifecycle: Estate Planning.

QUESTIONS TO ASK BEFORE YOU PROGRESS TO THE NEXT PHASE:

1. If you want to, have you expanded, franchised or licensed your business?
2. Are all of your systems, processes and procedures in place?
3. Do you have a product that other business owners want to use?

CHAPTER 8

Phase 8 – Estate Planning

Let's face it; everyone is going to die at some point in their life. Unsurprisingly, estate planning is a task that most business owners do not want to consider; for that matter most people do not want to consider what is going to happen when they die or if they become incapacitated. The Estate Planning phase of the Business Legal Lifecycle is about looking to the future and what will happen with your business, assets and family when you die or if you become unable to continue working in the business.

As unpleasant as it may be, you need to take action as early on in the Business Legal Lifecycle as possible. However, you will so often be caught up in running and building your business that you don't have time to take the necessary precautions for an event that may not happen for a long time. This is the reason why I have put this phase at this stage of the Business Legal Lifecycle. Once you have a sustainable business, you have a valuable asset you need to protect in the event of your death or incapacity to protect your family and business partner(s). Ideally, the Estate Planning phase should be done much earlier but the Business Legal Lifecycle is a realistic model and I have found that in the overwhelming majority of cases, it is best for this phase to occur at this point in the Business Legal Lifecycle.

Key aspects of estate planning include:

- Wills
- Testamentary trusts
- Powers of attorney
- Advanced health decisions
- Personal insurance
- Buy/sell option agreements

Important considerations during this phase are:

- How do I want to be remembered?
- What knowledge will I pass on to the next generation?

- How will I pass on my wealth and business to the next generation?
- How do I protect my family if something happens to me?

Dangerous considerations during this phase are:

- I do not want to think about what happens if I die or become disabled
- My family will sort it all out when something happens to me
- I do not need assistance because my family is independently wealthy

8.1 Wills

A will is a document that sets out your plans for your assets, possessions and belongings when you pass away. One of the main reasons that people avoid having a will is that they don't want to think about the inevitable. Your business, however, is your legacy so you should decide what happens to it, rather than letting others decide for you. One common misconception is that people think that if they pass away, their immediate family, in particular their spouse or civil partner, will receive their estate and there will be no disputes. This very rarely happens, especially where multiple parties are entitled to a share of an inheritance.

In the United States, if you die without a valid will in place, you will die 'intestate'. Different states have different rules dealing with the situation where you die without a will. In Florida, for example, if you die intestate and leave a surviving spouse, or civil partner, and children (including those from a previous marriage or relationship), your estate will be divided according to a specific distribution list under the intestacy provisions of the probate laws in Florida. For example:

(a) Your spouse will receive half of your estate and a life estate in the homestead property (the definition of Homestead Property in this context is very specific to Florida; you need to consult with your local attorney to ensure how this rule may apply to you).

(b) The remainder of your estate will be divided amongst your descendants, and the descendants will also receive a vested remainder in the homestead property.

These provisions vary depending on which state you live in and can be altered by special elections which your heirs may have a right to make.

Many people are surprised by the intestacy rules as they do not realize the implications of what happens if they pass away without a will. It is critical that, at a bare minimum, you have a will in place that sets out what you want to happen with your estate when you die. You should consult with your attorney, financial advisors and business advisors before your will is prepared to ensure that your wishes are properly expressed and documented.

You need to be careful here; if you change your mind on any point, you may well need to draft an entirely new will.

8.2 Power of Attorney and Advanced Health Decisions

The term 'Power of Attorney' is used, in this context, to describe a document that grants one person the right to deal with the financial and/or personal and health matters of another person. The Power of Attorney operates whilst a person is alive and ceases upon their death (as their will or the rules relating to intestacy take over at that point).

A Power of Attorney is most commonly granted between spouses to ensure that if something happens to one, the other can deal with matters on their behalf. A Power of Attorney also usually deals with financial matters, such as banking, property and shares, as well as health matters, such as making care decisions and choice of doctors.

Before granting someone a Power of Attorney, it is vital that you seek advice from your attorney and other financial advisors to ensure that you understand what powers you are granting to another party and what may happen in the event that the power is exercised once granted, the power can usually only be withdrawn through the signing of a specific document withdrawing the Power of Attorney.

An advanced health decision is a document that lists a variety of medical conditions and your instructions as to what you want done if you are afflicted by that condition. Ideally, it should be completed with the assistance of a qualified medical practitioner so that you understand the implications of the listed medical conditions, its likely effects and treatment options so you can make informed decisions regarding your future care.

It is critical, however, that these documents are drafted and reviewed by your attorney to ensure that they comply with specific legal requirements, including signing the document, witnesses and proper form. You also need to ensure that the originals are stored in a safe place and that your family and/or friends are able to access them if they are needed.

8.3 Personal Insurance

Personal insurance, as distinct from other business insurances discussed in section 2.6, pay out in the event of your death, disability or some other disastrous event occurring. Some people feel they do not need insurance as nothing will happen to them or that they are independently wealthy and do not need to have insurance. You should be aware, however, that if you are unfortunate enough to suffer a catastrophic event, it will have a drastic effect on your business, your family's ability to earn an income, and/or the level of care that they are able to maintain.

There are various types of personal insurance including:

(a) Life or Accidental Death insurance – usually pays a lump sum to a beneficiary when a person dies

(b) Total and permanent disability insurance – which can either pay out a lump sum or as periodic payments where a person suffers an injury or an illness that prevents them from being able to work

There are many other forms of insurance and types of cover that can be obtained depending on your situation and profile including critical illness insurance, long-term care insurance and health insurance. If you are considering personal insurance, you should discuss your options with your financial planner or business insurance providers to ensure you're properly covered and understand the circumstances under which you may or may not make a claim (e.g. extent of injuries needed to be deemed permanently disabled).

From the Case Files

An example of the benefit of having this type of insurance was where a business owner suffered a debilitating disease that forced her to be in and out of hospital for two years. The business in question was a large commercial real estate agency that had a significant sales business and a very large commercial rent roll. When the owner of the business fell ill the business suffered significantly as she was the backbone of the business. However, as she had the right insurance policy, the insurance company paid a periodic payment to top up the business owner's income for a significant period to cover the losses that the business suffered. This allowed the business owner to maintain her family and ensure that they worked through the illness and did not lose their business or other assets.

Sadly, there are many examples of where not having this insurance has forced a business owner to either sell their business at a great loss or, even worse, lose their business entirely. Personal insurances may seem expensive but they are there to protect you in unforeseen circumstances. You should ensure that you have proper insurance to protect you and your business and you should consult with your financial planner and accountant to make sure that you have the right policies in place for your needs.

8.4 Option Agreements

When you are in business with a business partner, it is vital to consider the consequences and effect on the business if something happens to one of you including illness, death, desire to sell out or retirement. It is important that you plan for the future of your business to ensure that a proper succession plan is in place so the business can continue with a minimum of disruption.

The best way to deal with such matters is for the partners to enter into a call option agreement. This agreement is often included in a shareholders' agreement, discussed at section 6.3. An agreement is a contract entered into between business partners whereby they agree that if one partner dies or is unable to continue in the business, the surviving partner(s) is bound to buy out the other party's share in the business. Specific events that may trigger a call option agreement include death, long-term disability, retirement or bankruptcy.

One problem of these types of arrangements is that quite often, the price for the share will often be cost or cash flow prohibitive. At times when clients have approached me for advice on such a matter, I have usually recommended that all partners obtain personal insurance (as discussed in section 8.3) that will pay out a sum of money to the remaining partner(s) which can be used to purchase the business share in question.

On the death of its owner, a business may be either:

- gifted to the intended recipient via a will
- sold via an option agreement

A call agreement, however, will take precedence over a will because the business will be transferred pursuant to the contract, triggered by the death or disability of one of the business owners. A properly drafted buy/sell option agreement will take the stress out of this aspect of the partner's death/disability and ensure that the surviving partner(s) are not forced to remain in the business against their will.

<u>From the Case Files</u>

An example of where this did not work was a large mechanics business which had a turnover of over $3 million a year, significant commitments with various premises, and a large number of team members to operate the business. The business was owned by two friends and one of the duo suddenly died. Overnight, the business lost a significant amount of its capacity and also had to deal with grieving team members and family. The deceased's family decided that they wanted to stay in the business after his death. The surviving business owner was then forced to be in business with people that he did not know or particularly like. As a result of this forced partnership, the business suffered significantly, closing various premises and being left in a situation where they could no longer operate. Eventually, the business folded and the parties were left with nothing as they could not work together. Had the original partners put an option agreement in place, the surviving business owner would have been able to take over the business and continue to operate in exchange for the deceased partner's estate receiving a cash payment for their portion of the business.

8.5 Conclusion

Dealing with your estate in the event of your death or disability is of critical importance to you as a business owner. If you don't deal with it, your family, friends and business partners could be left to clean up a mess that could have been easily avoided with properly drafted documentation.

Once you die or are disabled and cannot communicate properly, you will lose control over what happens to your business, so in order to ensure that your business is not affected any more than absolutely necessary, you need the correct documentation in place. More importantly, you need to make sure that your family is protected so that they do not have something else to worry about on top of your death or disability.

You need to consult with your attorney, accountant, financial planner and other business advisors on these topics to ensure that they all work together to document and carry out your wishes correctly. It is also critical that you review these documents at least every two years as situations change. They are not documents that can be drafted and then forgotten about for 20 or 30 years; they require constant appraisal and consideration to ensure that your legacy goes where you want it to go.

I have seen many business owners fail to do this properly because they did not want to consider their own mortality. However, what I see is that where a business owner does consider this phase properly, they take the time to get the right advice and follow it. This is a relief to them as they know that their family and business will be dealt with in the way that they want them to be in the case of their death or disability. Once these protections are put in place you are then ready to enter the next phase of the Lifecycle, Investing in Property.

QUESTIONS TO ASK BEFORE YOU PROGRESS TO THE NEXT PHASE:

1. Do you have a will in place?
2. Do you have a Power of Attorney in place?
3. Where you have a business partner, do you have a call option agreement in place?
4. Do these documents properly outline what you want to happen to your estate when you die?
5. Is your family protected in the case whereby something happens to you?
6. Is your business protected in the case whereby something happens to you?

CHAPTER 9

Phase 9 – Investing in Property

Now that you have a business that is successful and making lots of money, you need to consider what to do with your profits. The worst thing you can do is to squander your hard-earned money on consumer goods or fritter your money away on throwaway items. You need to consider your future and the best way to assure your financial security so that you have the money and time to enjoy your life. You want to have the option to work if you want to, not because you have to.

One strategy that is popular with successful investors over many years is the purchase of real property as an income producing asset. I use the term 'real property' here to refer to physical land or buildings. There are many other investments that you may choose to invest in, such as shares, but the purpose of this phase involves real property as the most appropriate investment for most business owners at this phase of the Business Legal Lifecycle.

There are many different types of property to buy:

(a) Your own home

(b) Residential property

(c) Commercial property

(d) Industrial property

(e) Units

(f) Townhouses

All property has benefits and risks. It is not the purpose of this book to go through each type or to give financial advice. While my personal preference is to invest in property given its long-term history of building equity, return and reward, I understand why people like to invest in other types of assets. As your business generates more profits, you should consider investing in property to ensure that you can build an investment portfolio of passive investments (although property is not *strictly* a passive investment, it is generally considered to be so) that can pay you an income without your active involvement. You should treat your investments as a separate business which is funded by your successful primary business.

This phase is located on the upward trend of the Business Legal Lifecycle as it is all about protecting your future as a business owner. However, I have observed that when a business reaches this phase, you need to consider investing in property now otherwise you will never do so or worse still will not do so properly, which could have a dramatic effect on your ability to set yourself up for the future phases in the Business Legal Lifecycle.

In this section I will discuss the considerations for buying residential, commercial and industrial property, the general process of buying a property, important factors that may impact the buying decision, questions to ask the real estate agent and strategies for selling property.

Important considerations during this phase are:

- What are my goals in life?
- Where do I see myself in 20 to 30 years?
- What is my risk profile and am I willing to take investment risks that may result in losing some of my savings?

Dangerous considerations during this phase are:

- I do not have the money to invest
- I am too scared to borrow
- I can borrow lots and lots of money

9.1 Buying Residential Property

Buying property can be an emotional experience, whether it's a residence in which you intend to live or an investment. It is crucial, however, that any investment purchase decision you make is made with a clear, objective and unemotional mind. Important considerations to keep in mind include:

- The fair and reasonable market value for the property
- How you will pay for the purchase
- The amount you will borrow, the interest rate and fees that will be charged and how you will service your debt
- The potential income your investment is generating currently and in the future

- Rental conditions in the area in which your investment property is located
- Whether the property is positively or negatively geared
- Current renovations needed and future upkeep costs

All of these considerations are important for a person looking at investing in residential real estate. In the purchase of any property there are a range of matters to consider so this list is made up of common considerations that I consider to be relevant when people make such investment.

From the Case Files

An example of this type of investment was a client who enjoyed large profits in their successful accounting practice that had a number of different businesses and turned over significant revenue of over $5 million per year. The accountant knew that he did not want to work as an accountant forever (even though he was very good at it) and decided to invest his money rather than spending it on consumable items. He bought a large number of residential properties with a moderate rental return so that he was able to generate an income from these properties to be able to pay for his family's lifestyle. He was then able to choose when he wanted to work as he did not need the money but rather was able to have that freedom because he was disciplined in his investments.

9.2 Buying Commercial/Industrial Property

The same considerations apply when buying a commercial or industrial property, as well as additional considerations such as the potential for a greater return measured against the greater risk of vacancy, and the type and location of the property depending on its location. Even where the property has a long-term commercial or industrial business as a tenant, caution should be used to ensure that the tenant does not leave, causing the investment to backfire and costing you more money than it was worth.

Another type of purchase involves the purchase of premises from which your business operates. The obvious advantage is that instead of paying rent, you are building a business asset. This means that you are not paying rent to another property owner and you are building your own property portfolio for your benefit. Of course there are risks in doing this as, if your business fails, you will also lose the income from your business to the investment aspects of your property portfolio business.

9.3 The Process of Buying a Property

The process of buying a property is called conveyancing. Different conveyancing processes are utilized around the world, so always seek local legal advice to ensure that you follow the correct procedures. The conveyancing process is similar throughout the different states in the US. The process in Florida is generally as follows:

(a) Prospective buyers inspect a property for sale to make a decision about whether to attempt to buy the property from the seller. This is usually done with a realtor as they have access to the Multiple Listing Service (MLS).

(b) Ordinarily, a buyer will make an offer to the seller in a private sale and the seller then has the choice to accept or reject the offer, or attempt to negotiate a different deal with the buyer.

(c) Once a purchase price is agreed, the buyer and the seller sign a contract for the sale of land, which will include all of the improvements (such as buildings) on the land; this is usually prepared by the realtor (or attorney) (usually the buyer and the seller will receive copies of the signed contract, at which point a deposit, for example 10% of the total purchase price, will be paid).

(d) The parties each appoint a closing agent to handle the conveyancing process; this is usually the title company that issues title insurance on the property. The title company should explain to their client the various obligations and rights placed on their client as a result of signing the contracts. The attorney (or title company) should also explain what must be done by the buyer in order to ensure that the buyer is able to close the transfer of the property.

(e) The term 'close' or 'closing' refers to the time that the buyer actually pays the purchase price to the seller and the seller actually transfers the property to the buyer.

(f) The title company provides all of the required legal documents to close the transfer of the property. The attorney (or title company) also ensures that the legal documents are signed, as necessary, by the parties to the transaction.

(g) Ordinarily the title company or closing agent will also record a document known as a deed to the property. The purpose of this document is to prevent the seller from transferring the property to a third party unknown to the buyer.

(h) The attorney (or title company) conducts searches through numerous government records to ensure that the property is as it appears and that there are no problems that need to be addressed pursuant to the terms of the contract.

It is important that you engage a competent and experienced attorney (or title company) so that they can properly review these searches so that your rights are protected.

(i) The attorney (or title company) communicates with banks and other parties to ensure that everything and everyone is coordinated for, and on, the day of the closing.

As can be seen from this very brief outline of the steps to be taken in the conveyancing process, the process is a complicated one with a variety of steps required to ensure that the parties comply with both the terms of the contract and the legislation governing the process.

9.4 Important Factors to Consider when Buying a Property

There are a number of important considerations that a property investor needs to think about before making a decision to purchase. The following is a list of standard elements of the transaction you must consider prior to entering into the contract to purchase a property:

- Entity – what entity or vehicle are you going to use to buy the property? The various types of entities are discussed in section 2.1. You should take the advice of your attorney, accountant and financial planner in relation to these matters as there will be significant legal and financial implications depending on your decision.

- Purchase price – it is important when buying a property that you consider the purchase price properly; not only in terms of affordability and market rate but also as part of your overall investment strategy.

- Deposit – The deposit is the amount that is paid to the stakeholder (usually the agent) and can be forfeited to the seller if the buyer defaults under the contract. Generally, a deposit for the purchase of property should be no more than 10% of the purchase price. This is distinct from the deposit (or equity, or loan to value percentage) required by any bank that is funding your purchase. Depending on the type of property and your history with the bank they may require that you put up your own funds of up to 20% to 40% of the purchase price as a deposit on your loan.

- Mortgage – it is important to consider how you are going to be able to afford to purchase the property. If you are going to borrow money from a mortgage lender, you must ensure that the contract is subject to obtaining finance approval from a bank or other financial institution.

- Building and surveyors – when buying a property, you should always make the contract subject to a satisfactory building inspection/survey.

- What do you do if an encumbrance (mortgage or charge) is against the property (other than the vendor's mortgage)? An encumbrance is definitely something that you should be concerned about. If an encumbrance is registered, then you should ask the agent for an explanation of what it is about and then seek advice from your attorney (or conveyancer) as it may adversely affect the property you are buying.

- Is the property leased? If it is then you need to ensure that you know when the lease ends and what rent is being received. The question of when the lease ends is important if you want to live in the property yourself. On the other hand, if you are looking to buy an investment property, a lease will affect your return on the investment if the tenant leaves. You should also consider the tenants that are in the property and the deposit that is held. This may be important depending on the tenants and how much work may be required to rectify any damage to the property caused by the tenants.

- Special conditions – depending on your circumstances or the condition of the property, you may require special conditions (for example, easements) to be written into the contract. Some agents will draft their own special conditions; however, it is always advisable that you check these conditions with your attorney to ensure the effect of the clause is in accordance with your requirements.
- Completion – there are a number of factors that determine when the parties close the contract. It is common practice to close the purchase of the property at least 30 days from the date of exchange of contracts.

9.5 What Questions are Important to ask the Real Estate Agent?

There are many questions that are important to ask the real estate agent before you sign the contract to buy a property. The number and type of questions will vary depending on the property that is being considered for purchase and also your experience in buying property. Generally, you should ask:

(a) **How long has the property been on the market?**

This question is going to give you an idea of how keen the seller is to sell. It is difficult to provide any definitive plan of attack to take from the answer; however, most sellers become more eager to sell their home the longer it is on the market. Once a property has been for sale for six to eight weeks, many sellers (and agents) start to think that their selling price is too high. If the agent states that the property has been on the market for at least six weeks, ask the agent if the price has been already reduced or whether the seller would consider a reduced price less than the listed price (where a listed price is given).

(b) **Will the seller negotiate on price?**

This may sound ridiculous, but do not underestimate its power. By asking this question an agent might just give up the information you want to know before you make an offer.

(c) **Why is the seller selling?**

Knowing the answer to this question can give you an indication in relation to how eager the seller will be to sell. This may enable you to work out their timetable or deadline for selling. For example, if the agent tells you that they are moving to another location to start work in four weeks, you know they are motivated to sell as soon as possible. Whereas if they are downsizing because the kids have left home and they still have not bought a new place to live, they may be willing to hold out longer to get a higher price.

(d) **Have they had any offers so far and, if so, how much?**

This is an important question to find out whether any previous offers have been made, and what amounts have been declined, or offers that have been accepted but possibly fallen through. This can give you an idea of what purchase price the seller will accept, and also give you an indication as to what price other potential buyers believe the property is worth.

(e) **What is the lowest price that the seller will accept?**

As an agent acts on behalf of a seller, they will not usually tell you this information, but it is worth asking to see what the answer is. For example, if an agent says, 'they'll take $450,000', you know not to make an offer over this amount. Even if they do not give you an exact amount, they are likely to give you an indication as to the price that the seller may be willing to accept.

This is not an exhaustive list of questions; however, from my experience with buying and selling property, these are important questions to ask in relation to the purchase of any property. Other questions may involve information about the property, and whether the agent is aware of any changes in the area that may affect the value or amenity of the property (such as whether infrastructure is being considered or being built that may increase or decrease the traffic flow in the area).

The exact consequences of these types of questions depend on the circumstances and you should always have your attorney verify any information of this nature that is provided by the agent, as the agent may not be aware of all proposals in the area that may affect your decision to buy the property. Buying property is an important consideration for any person including business owners.

It is important that you seek advice from consultants such as your attorney, accountants, financial planners, business coaches, life coaches, mortgage brokers, and real estate agents to ensure that you buy the right property and follow the process properly. Having the right agent can make an extraordinary difference: an example is when a client was selling a commercial property with an existing business onsite. The property had been up for sale for a long time with no luck until the new agent appointed by the seller was able to, due to his experience and business acumen, put together a package attractive to investors. The property was sold within four weeks.

9.6 Selling Property (be it Residential, Commercial or Industrial)

Any investment can be sold and there are a number of important considerations that any seller, in particular business owners, need to give to the sale of their properties. The process is similar to that described in sections 9.1 – 9.4; however, when you sell your property you will need to ensure that you appoint the right real estate agent to sell your property. Some important questions to ask are:

(a) **How long has the agent been practicing?**

The answer to this question will give you an idea about the person that you are appointing but it is critical to remember that just because your agent is more experienced does not necessarily mean that they will sell your property faster or for more money than a less experienced agent. More significantly is whether they have access to competent mentors and their level of training.

(b) **What is the best marketing plan or strategy for my needs?**

You will need to ask the agent:

(i) Specifically, how will you sell my property?

(ii) What is your direct mail campaign and which platform do you use? And who are your clients? Do you use the MLS?

(iii) Where and how often do you advertise?

(iv) Will you show me a sample flyer?

(v) How do you market online?

(vi) Will you please provide references?

Everybody has references; even new agents have references from previous employers. So ask to see references and confirm that the referees given are not related to the agent and that they can be contacted with additional questions.

(c) **What are the top three things that separate the agent from their competition?**

A good agent will not hesitate to answer this question and will be ready to fire off why they are best suited to sell your property. Every person has their own set of standards, but most consumers say they are looking for agents who are:

(i) Honest and trustworthy

(ii) Assertive

(iii) Excellent negotiators

(iv) Available by phone or email

(v) Good communicators

(vi) Friendly

(vii) Analytical

(viii) Able to maintain a good sense of humor under trying circumstances

(d) **May I review documents beforehand that I will be asked to sign?**

Generally, when appointing an agent, you will need to sign documents such as:

(i) Agency disclosure

(ii) Listing agreement

You should review these documents thoroughly and obtain advice before signing anything.

(e) **How will the agent help me find other professionals?**

Let the agent explain to you who they work with and why they choose particular professionals. Your agent should be able to supply you with a written list of referrals such as attorneys.

Ask for an explanation if you see the term 'affiliated' because it could mean that the agent is receiving compensation from one or all of the vendors engaged as a result of the referral, and you could be paying a premium for the service.

(f) **How much does the agent charge?**

Do not ask if the fee is negotiable. All real estate fees are negotiable. You should negotiate a fair fee for the service that they are going to provide.

(g) **What kind of guarantee does the agent offer?**

If you sign an agency agreement and later decide that you are unhappy with the arrangement, will the agent let you cancel the agreement? Will the agent stand behind their service to you? What is their company's policy about canceled agreements? Has anybody ever canceled an agreement with them before? If so, why?

(h) **What haven't I asked the agent that I need to know?**

Pay close attention to how the agent answers this question because there is always something you need to know; always. You want an agent to take their time with you to make sure you feel comfortable and secure with their knowledge and experience.

Appointing an agent to sell a property is a big decision and all factors are important. You need to carefully consider all of these aspects and trust your instincts with regards to engaging the right agent to sell your property.

I have advised many clients in relation to the sale of their property. It takes skill to sell property and I know that many different agents will try to say that they can sell property in any circumstances.

One example was a client who wanted to sell his residential property; he asked the questions outlined above and was able to achieve a quick sale of his property due to selecting the right agent. A lot of the selection process will be your gut feelings and in most cases you should trust your intuition based on the answers to the above questions.

9.7 Conclusion

Investing in property is a very important phase in the Business Legal Lifecycle. This phase is all about setting you up for the future by ensuring that your business feeds into the other aspects of your life.

This will give you security going into the future and through the final phases of the Business Legal Lifecycle. It is imperative that any person, including business owners, obtain appropriate advice before embarking on this phase.

Not doing so can have disastrous consequences and can end up costing you a lot of money in the future to get right or fix. I have found that business owners who follow these steps feel that they are comfortable about the future and ready to tackle whatever comes next. It also creates, in the business owner, a sense of relief that they are setting themselves and their families up for the future.

Once you have the right advice from your various consultants, you will find that you are in a great place to be able to successfully navigate your way through this phase of the Business Legal Lifecycle.

You will then be ready to move onto the next phase, Litigation, knowing that you are starting to be financially secure.

QUESTIONS TO ASK BEFORE YOU PROGRESS TO THE NEXT PHASE:

1. What are your investment goals?
2. Where will these investments take you in the next 20 to 30 years?
3. What type of property do you want to invest in?
4. Do you understand the process?
5. Are you willing to take investment risks that may result in losing some of your savings?

CHAPTER 10

Phase 10 – Litigation and Dispute Resolution

Litigation is the term that is given to the process that involves either commencing proceedings in a court to sue someone or defending an action in a court. Dispute resolution is the term given to the efforts made to reach a resolution to a dispute before it gets to litigation. The Litigation and Dispute Resolution phase is positioned at this point of the Business Legal Lifecycle due to the fact that no matter how successful your business is, it is likely you will encounter some form of litigation during the Lifecycle. Different types of litigation that could threaten a business include:

(a) Debt recovery – this is the process that you need to follow to recover a bad debt. As I said earlier (see section 3.6) this may come up earlier in the Business Legal Lifecycle

(b) Intellectual property disputes – this may occur when someone uses your intellectual property without your consent

(c) Other actions brought forward for more complicated disputes

In the Litigation phase, I will go through the basics of litigation, some tips on avoiding litigation, some tips on debt recovery, and matters to consider if you are being sued.

Going to court is not a pleasant experience for any business owner. It means that something has gone terribly wrong in a business relationship that cannot be resolved by negotiation or discussion. Statistically speaking, only one in every thousand disputes results in litigation and, of these, less than 5% will proceed as far as a trial. Even though only a miniscule amount of disputes actually end up in court, it is important that you understand the process, as avoiding it will save a great deal of time and money.

Important considerations during this phase are:

- Is there anything I can do to avoid going to court?
- Do I have a strong case?
- What are my rights?

- How much is it going to cost to go to court?
- How do I mediate to resolve the dispute quickly?
- Once I am in court what do I do?
- How can I recover the money owed to me?

Dangerous considerations during this phase are:

- I don't need legal advice
- I know my rights and can act for myself
- They will pay eventually (if it is a debt)
- I do not need to do anything as the dispute will resolve itself or they will go away

10.1 What is Litigation?

Litigation is the term used to describe the court process to resolve disputes. Generally, litigation involves the following (summarized):

(a) A dispute between two or more parties

(b) The aggrieved party (plaintiff or claimant) initiates proceedings in a court by filing a statement of claim with a court

(c) The defending party (defendant) will file a defense to the plaintiff's statement of claim. If the defendant feels they have been wronged as well, they can also file a counterclaim. If the defendant does not defend the proceedings, then the plaintiff can, by default, obtain a judgment against the defendant

(d) The plaintiff must defend any counterclaim against them, otherwise the counterclaim may succeed

(e) The parties exchange arguments and evidence (additional information may be requested by either party) and usually at this point the court will require that the parties attend a mediation or conference in an attempt to resolve the dispute

(f) If the dispute is not resolved by mediation, then it goes to a hearing by an impartial independent third party (such as a judge or jury)

(g) Judgment is handed down upon deciding the result of the dispute (subject to an appeal). If the judgment is not appealed, the successful party can seek to enforce it against the unsuccessful party including:

   (i) bringing the unsuccessful party into court to question them about what assets they own

   (ii) if the unsuccessful party owns real or personal property, the successful party can usually take steps to sell that property to recover the amount of the judgment

   (iii) attacking money held in the bank account of the unsuccessful party

   (iv) if the unsuccessful party is a company, the successful party can look to 'wind up' the unsuccessful party (see section 13.2)

   (v) if the unsuccessful party is a person, the successful party can look to 'bankrupt' the unsuccessful party (see section 13.3)

There are other steps that a successful party can take to enforce their judgment but these are the most useful that I have seen to enforce a judgment for a debt. As can be seen from this short explanation, the process of litigation is a lengthy one that will incur significant costs. It is critically important that any person engaging in litigation ascertain from their attorney what the implications, consequences and costs are likely to be before making a decision whether the action is worth pursuing or defending. They also need to be aware that, if they lose, they will likely to be liable for a lot of additional costs from the successful party.

<u>From the Case Files</u>

An example of where a client did not understand the process was when they were using another attorney for litigation. The client was a franchisor of a large franchise business that sold various food products to the public in a large number of stores. The business had not had any disputes with their franchisees for many years; 20 in fact, that they had been operating a franchise business. However, at one point the client entered into a dispute with a franchisee. The client did not have the process explained to them or the likely costs of entering into the litigation. An assumption was made by the attorney that the client understood the process and the likely costs and timing. This was made worse by the fact that the client had been in business for a long period of time so the attorney presumed that they had been through the litigation process before. Unfortunately, the client did not understand the process and at mediation had the opportunity to resolve the dispute and pay the franchisee $50,000.00. As the franchisor did not understand the process and the fact that they could lose, they went to trial and were forced to pay $600,000.00. Had the process been explained to them clearly they would have resolved the matter much earlier and for far less money. In the end the franchisor paid the money and was able to continue trading but after suffering a significant loss as a result of not understanding either the process or the risks involved.

10.2 Dispute Resolution

Avoiding litigation as far as possible is always the smart move. Not only is litigation a costly process, but it can also be a mentally and physically draining process as well. Choosing the right litigation strategy and understanding how to avoid litigation through dispute resolution can save you a lot of money. Strategies include:

(a) Taking a step back in the dispute – by taking a calm, commercial view of the matter, the chance that the parties might resolve the dispute without litigation will increase

(b) Understanding the process will encourage you to mediate a resolution as it is going to cost thousands of dollars even if you are successful in understanding that once the court makes a decision, it is final – and you could lose. By making a commercial settlement early, the parties gain some certainty and control over the outcome

(c) By agreeing on the smaller points first, the chance of the parties finding middle ground is increased. Often, the quickest way to resolve a dispute is for the parties to start to agree on some smaller points which can lead to further agreements being made between the parties which can snowball into a resolution of the dispute

(d) Where the parties cannot find any common ground, they should at the very least try to agree on the exact scope of the dispute, and what issues will be required to resolve it on behalf of both parties

(e) Appointing a trusted, impartial third party to attempt to mediate a resolution to the dispute

(f) Trying to understand the other party's perspective. Most disputes come from a misunderstanding and, by putting oneself in the other person's shoes, the parties may see a way through the dispute and come to a resolution

(g) Arbitration, which is becoming a more popular form of dispute resolution. It is often used in commercial disputes. In essence, arbitration is a dispute resolution hearing where a third party arbitrator or arbitrators will sit in a tribunal and decide the correct outcome of a dispute. Arbitration is an alternative to court action, and generally is just as final and binding as a court decision.

From the Case Files

An example of when these techniques worked well was when our client, a large property developer, entered into a contract to purchase a property to redevelop as part of a large managed investment plan that operated different projects. The property owners were a couple who did not understand contracts or how to handle disputes and, unfortunately, neither did their attorney. The contract contained a term whereby our client was allowed to remove a tree on the property before settlement. This was required as our client wanted to make an application to the relevant City Council to develop the property. If the application was made with the tree on the property, the Council may have forced our client to retain the tree and our client wanted it removed. Due to a misunderstanding between the attorney and the property owners, permission was given to our client without the knowledge of the property owners to remove the tree. The property owners tried to negotiate a change to the conditions by placing strict conditions on our client entering the property. Rather than going to court, the parties were able to negotiate a resolution that was acceptable to both parties, the tree was removed and the property was redeveloped as required by our client.

I have always taken the view that it is in a business owner's interest to avoid litigation as far as possible for the reasons set out in this chapter. Sometimes it is unavoidable, but every effort should be made to avoid litigation and only use it as a last resort.

10.3 Debt Recovery

Cash flow is the lifeblood of any business. Often businesses are crippled when they are owed large sums of money by clients that are either slow to make payments or refuse to pay the debt altogether. When a business reaches this phase, it is imperative that the business has policies and procedures in place to recover those debts efficiently. The debt recovery process can either be undertaken internally or outsourced to a debt collection agency or attorney. Whichever method you choose, it is important that you set clearly defined payment terms to ensure that your cash flow is maintained at a level sufficient to allow you to operate your business.

Generally, debt recovery is something that happens before litigation, which should only be used as a last resort option. Before beginning any debt recovery action, you must ensure that you are not spending more money than you are going to recover. In dealing with any bad debt, it is important that a business owner or their employees:

- Knows all of the details about the person that owes the money to the business
- Approaches the debtor with confidence
- Are always business-like and courteous when dealing with a debtor
- Listen carefully and adapt their approach accordingly
- Convey a sense of urgency in setting deadlines for payments
- Be calm and cheerful no matter how rude the debtor may become
- Make sure the debtor knows you want a fair outcome

By following these simple guidelines, you will show the debtor that you are serious about collecting the debt. Becoming aggressive and rude will only escalate any conflict between the parties and it is unlikely to result in a favorable resolution.

Debt collection is vitally important for any business. If you choose to appoint a third party to collect the debt on your behalf, it is important that you choose the right debt collection agent. In doing so, you should ensure that the agent is properly registered and complies with any prescribed laws that may restrict their practices. If you choose to collect your own debts, there are a variety of processes freely available on the internet. You should have your processes reviewed by your attorney to ensure that you are complying with all applicable laws.

From the Case Files

An example of where these procedures and a strict compliance worked was a large law firm that had approximately 120 employees and an annual turnover close to $10 million per year. They had significant debtors owing in excess of $1 million across a number of clients. The law firm did not have a debt collection policy; rather they had a policy whereby each attorney was responsible for chasing up their own debts. Unfortunately for the law firm, the attorneys never had time to chase debts as they were too busy working on the next case. The firm decided to implement a strict debt collection strategy and procedure. They followed the procedures and the law firm was able to ensure that they had no bad debts owing for more than 30 days. The advantage for the firm was that they had instantly increased operating cash flow which allowed the owners to take a greater profit from the business.

10.4 Defending Proceedings Brought against a Business

Where proceedings have commenced or threatened to commence against your business, it is critical that you obtain advice from your attorney immediately. Action may be commenced against you in a number of ways, including:

(a) Via a letter of demand or a statement with a message threatening that proceedings will be commenced if a debt is not paid

(i) if you or your business owe the money and there is no dispute or counterclaim then the best thing to do is to pay the debt

(ii) if you do not have the money and there is no dispute or counterclaim, then the next best course of action is to contact the creditor and ask for time to pay as per a reasonable payment plan. If there is a dispute or counterclaim, then you should discuss this point with the creditor and attempt to resolve the dispute amicably. If there is a difference (for example, the debtor believes that they owe $50 but the creditor is saying that they are owed $70), then pay the amount that the debtor believes is owing so that the amount left is all that there is a dispute about

(b) If proceedings have been commenced then you need to consider exactly what you want to do, including:

(i) whether to dispute the debt or to pay it (usually plus costs and interest)

(ii) if you choose to dispute the debt and do not want to pay it, then you should consult with an attorney immediately to ensure that the proper paperwork is filed to protect you against any sort of judgment, as well as exploring the other options for settlement

From the Case Files

An example with a negative outcome was where a business owner was sued for the non-payment of a debt that was owed for the supply of materials required for the business. The business was a large company that manufactured bull bars and supplied them to multiple different truck companies to sell with their vehicles. The business owner owed money to a number of suppliers of the material that was used to make the bull bars to the sum of approximately $500,000.00. Rather than address the creditor the business owner simply put his head in the sand and did not want to deal with the issue as a result of cash flow issues. As the business owner did not seek advice at any time, he received a number of demand letters, and he even allowed proceedings to be commenced and nothing was done. It was only after judgment was obtained and enforcement proceedings were commenced (in this case it was an application to wind up the company that operated the business) did the business owner seek legal advice. The advice was the same as it would have been in the beginning: come to an arrangement to pay the debt and it will save the business from folding as a result of this debt. The creditor agreed to a reasonable payment plan which allowed the business owner to keep on trading out, pay the debt and also continue to receive materials from the supplier. Had he not taken these steps, the business would have folded. Coming to a late settlement meant that his debt was much higher (as it included costs and interest). The same payment option was open to the business owner from the beginning but, as he did not communicate with the other party at all, that decision cost him dearly.

A concerning trend amongst business owners is that instead of resolving a debt dispute quickly, they act as if (a) the dispute will go away, (b) decide that they will deal with it later or (c) hope that it will magically resolve itself. At the end of the day the best advice that I can give you is to deal with these matters head on. If you took a moment to put yourself in the shoes of your creditor, you would not appreciate delays in getting paid and the lack of communication, so treat your creditors the way you would want to be treated.

It is critical that before you respond to any actual or potential legal proceedings, you obtain advice from your attorney as to your rights, obligations and options after giving your financial circumstances due consideration. There are usually strict timeframes for responses to be made and, by not complying to those timeframes, you are leaving yourself exposed to having a judgment entered against you.

10.5 Conclusion

Litigation is a very important phase in the Business Legal Lifecycle and can have enormous ramifications on the future of your business. If the phase is not handled properly, it could potentially lead to the premature end of your business.

Failing this phase may force you to sell your business for much less than it is worth or, worse still, may result in seeing the next two phases (Sale of the Business and Retirement) skipped entirely, leading straight to the Insolvency/Winding Up phase. It is critical that you seek legal advice on all of these matters to ensure that you properly and safely navigate your way through it.

It is also important that you deal with all disputes in a commercial manner. Making sure that you are aware of the process, likely costs, and risks inherent in litigation will ensure that you make decisions on a financial, not emotional, basis.

Remember that in every dispute, there are always two sides and the truth usually lies somewhere in the middle.

Tackling debts head on is the best way for you to protect your business as you can find solutions that you can accept rather than having solutions imposed upon you by a court.

QUESTIONS TO ASK BEFORE YOU PROGRESS TO THE NEXT PHASE:

1. Have you paid all your debts that are due and owing?
2. If not, can you enter into a payment plan?
3. Is there anything that you can do to avoid going to court?
4. Do you have a strong case to go to court?
5. Do you understand the court process and the issues with going to court?
6. What are your rights?
7. How much is it going to cost to go to court?
8. Do you need to recover any debts owed to you?
9. Have you put debt collection procedures in place?

CHAPTER 11

Phase 11 – Sale of Whole or Part of the Business or the Listing on a Stock Exchange

Previously, I said that in acting for business owners, the Start-Up phase is the most exciting. Acting on behalf of a business owner in the sale of their profitable business is a close second. This phase is also rewarding as it is all about having a business that you can sell either as a whole, in part, or even listing it on a stock exchange or market.

This phase is often the culmination of all of the effort you put into your business over the years. The positioning of this phase is really due to its inherent nature. In every business, the goal is to build the most successful business possible irrespective of whether it is a lifestyle business that brings in an income to fund an ideal lifestyle, or a company with a turnover of over $10 million a year with appropriate consideration given to the possible sale of the business in the future.

This phase is at the top of the cycle as it represents the pinnacle of the business owner's involvement in the business. The best time to sell a business is when it reaches its optimum profitability, turnover and team capability. This does not mean that the business cannot become even more profitable, or that the buyer will then fail in the business. In fact, quite the opposite is often true; a good business that is at the top of its game can be sold to a buyer who then starts their own Business Legal Lifecycle and continues the success of the business.

A well-established business will already have a lot of the necessary processes and procedures in place, which will greatly assist the buyer (new business owner) to move forward.

The new owner may have to revisit the earlier phases in the Business Legal Lifecycle to familiarize themselves with the details of certain phases and to ensure that they are comfortable with the way in which the processes and procedures were set up by the previous business owner and make adjustments where necessary.

Sometimes, a business may be sold in less than ideal circumstances; ill-health, litigation or lack of funding may force a business owner away from their business. Of course, they do not have to sell their business as they may be prepared to sacrifice growth for a lifestyle business that will simply pay themselves a wage for the rest of their foreseeable lives.

The keyword here is 'foreseeable'; as discussed earlier there are many things outside the business owner's control that might force a business to be sold. In this phase of the Business Legal Lifecycle I will go through the key considerations that buyers have when looking at buying a business and what owners should have in place to maximize their selling price, irrespective of whether the sale is forced or by choice.

Important considerations during this phase are:

- If I wanted to buy this business what would I want?
- What are the unique things that make my business stand out?
- Have I protected my intellectual property?
- Have I completed the other phases of the Business Legal Lifecycle successfully?
- Are the financial books and records of my business up-to-date?
- Have I been taking any cash out of the business that will affect the bottom line of my business?
- Which consultants do I need to engage with to help me to sell my business?

Dangerous considerations during this phase are:

- My business is perfect; I do not need to do anything to get it sold
- I want $x for my business and what anyone else says does not matter
- I can negotiate on my own sale
- I do not need to bring my books and records up to date; they will be fine
- Everyone wants to buy my business

11.1 Taking Cash for Fees

At the start of this phase I wanted to address a matter which is often overlooked; owners taking money out of the business for personal reasons and without recording the profits. They do this for a number of reasons, including to avoid paying tax on the money, to hide money from their spouse or family law proceedings, or perhaps to hide money from their business partner.

The truth is that in any business, no person should be taking big risks for small gains; the tax man, your spouse or your business partner will inevitably find out that you have been hiding money from them and it will not end well. Not only could you end up with either a larger debt to the tax office (different countries around the world have different rules in relation to this; if you deliberately avoid paying certain taxes, that can attract significant penalties and interest), but you could have serious trust issues with your spouse or business partner.

However, the main reason you should not to take cash from your business is that for every $0.30 (depending on the current corporation tax rate), it could end up costing you $1, $3, or $5 when you sell your business. This is because when a business is sold, the sale price is generally calculated as a multiple of the profit made by the business (usually averaged over the previous two or three-year period). Profits need to be demonstrable so the prospective buyer can verify the purchase price. Therefore, for every dollar that you take out of your business, you could be short-changing yourself by much more when you sell your business.

For example, if you take $100,000.00 in cash from your business and then sold it you could not rely on that $100,000.00 as it is not recorded in the company books. Consequently, the company's value will be $300,000.00 less (based on a 3x multiple) than it should have been – quite a bit more than the $100,000.00 you took out initially. All of this is to save paying approximately $30,000.00 in company tax.

11.2 Selling a Business

In order to sell your business at your desired price, you need to ensure your business is a well-oiled machine that can work without you. The purpose of this book is not to go through every single aspect of selling your business, but to identify some of the major areas that help drive the price up when you sell your business. The process of selling a business is quite a complex one; it involves a great deal of high level negotiations and a number of important steps, including:

Having your business ready for sale

If you are considering selling your business you should engage a business broker, a valuer, and/or a business valuer to assist in the sale. The right consultant will not only be able to help you through the process but also to ensure that you receive the best possible price for your business.

Often, you will need to prepare an information memorandum (usually with the help of your advisors) that sets out the key investment considerations. This can include financial information, sales analyses, details of key personnel and descriptions of property. Sometimes this is within a virtual data room.

I have never seen a business with everything in place ready for sale at the time of asking. It generally takes about two years of discipline and hard work to get a business ready for sale. In many cases, a broker is not engaged to prepare a business for sale as the owner prefers to manage the sale personally.

Despite the owner's best efforts, they lack the specialist knowledge to extract maximum value from the sale, and often are unable to secure the sale as they cannot justify the asking price. In the end they are forced to accept a figure much lower than their asking price, abandon the sale, or go back to square one and hire a broker to get the job done properly.

<u>From the Case Files</u>

An example of this was a client who wanted to sell their service-based business. The business was a financial planning business that had a great revenue stream and was making solid profits of over $1 million per annum. The business owner met with a number of brokers who all told him that he needed to do significant work on the business to sell for the price that he wanted (being a 4x multiple of their profits). Despite this advice, the business owner decided that he did not want to engage a broker and that he would market the business himself for sale. The business was not ready for sale and the client marketed the business on a general website and did not engage a broker. He was serious about selling but every time a potential buyer came to him the client could not justify the price he wanted for the business. After marketing the business for six months, the business owner finally realized that he needed to engage the services of a broker. The broker spent some more time ensuring that the business was ready for sale and then started marketing the business. The business was sold after one month of marketing for a price greater than the business owner had initially wanted for the business.

The price

Before you sell your business you will, of course, have an idea of what you think it is worth. Invariably, the actual value will be less once the price of the business is actually calculated. Generally, the three main components that determine the price of a business are:

(a) the goodwill including intellectual property of the business

(b) any plant and equipment including digital assets of the business

(c) any stock or inventory that the business owns

The goodwill of the business

Goodwill is the real value and profit of the business and includes intellectual property; it is the key figure used in calculating a business's real worth. The goodwill of the business is generally worked out as a multiple of earnings before interest, tax, depreciation and amortization (EBITDA), or some variant, over a one, two or three-year period. What EBITDA calculates is the profit of the business before you add in any interest that you earn, take out any tax payments, or depreciate or amortize any assets.

The multiple is a figure that is attributed to how easily the business can be taken over and run without the current owner. The lower the multiple, the more reliant the business is on its owner; the higher the multiple, the more independent the business is from the owner, the better systems that the business has in place and the easier it is for a third party with no relatable experience to walk in and take over. Law and accounting firms, for example, generally have a low multiple as a large part of the goodwill is tied up in the personal relationships the practitioners have with their clients. Conversely a printing firm will have a much higher multiple as it is not so dependent on personal relationships.

Having systems in place and intellectual property protected is a great way to increase the multiple, meaning you are not needed in the daily operations of the business as much and it therefore becomes a more valuable and marketable asset.

Plant and equipment

The plant and equipment of the business are, put simply, the physical assets that are used to operate the business. In an office, for example, these might include the build out of the premises such as desks, chairs, filing cabinets, computers and telephones, while in a factory it might be the machinery and the ancillary items and equipment used to service the machinery. When a business is sold, the value of these items is calculated at the depreciated value of each asset (and rarely for its replacement value). Depreciated value is simply the loss in value of that asset over time.

Stock and inventory

Many businesses rely on stock and inventory to run the business; these are the products that are sold in the business or that are used to make products for the business to sell. When a business is sold, the source items that are used to make the product are generally sold at cost price. So, if the stock was bought at $1, it would be sold to the new buyer at $1 modified by the age and usefulness of the stock.

There are many considerations when looking at the price of a business; this is just a short summary of some of the factors you need to consider when selling your business. You should consult with a business broker, a valuer and/or a business valuer to ascertain the true value of your business and what price you will achieve in your market.

Marketing of the business for sale

Engaging a business broker to sell your business is the easiest way to market it to potential buyers. Generally, brokers will have a database of clients and customers that they can approach that may be interested in your business. They also have the ability and contacts to advertise your business in places where investors know to look when they are interested in buying a business.

The contract

A sale of business contract is a lot more complicated than a contract for the sale of land. It is important that the contract includes all things necessary to make the business continue to operate with the new owner, including:

(a) the name and address of the business

(b) the telephone, website, email addresses of the business

(c) any social media pages of the business

(d) the price that is agreed upon between the parties

(e) whether the contract is subject to any due diligence (that is, enquiries made in relation to the business to make sure that it is what the seller says it is), finance (to make sure that the buyer can buy the business) or any other inspections required by the buyer

(f) the transfer of any government licenses required to operate the business (e.g. liquor license)

(g) the transfer of the lease for the premises

(h) restraint of trade provisions, preventing the seller from operating a competing business or taking existing clients from the business

(i) any other aspect that is required for the business

If the vehicle that operates the business is set up correctly, then the tax position upon the sale of the business should be consistent with what was considered when the business was started (see section 2.1 on structures). You must obtain advice from your accountant and/or financial advisor as to your tax liability from the sale. There are often mechanisms that can be put into place to minimize the tax that you must pay upon the sale of your business.

You must also engage an attorney to either draft or review any business sale contract that you are considering entering into. For instance, you may be required to give certain types of disclosures when they are sold or when leases are being transferred. Therefore, it is essential that you obtain advice from a qualified attorney about the terms of the contract and that you tell your attorney about all aspects of the business to ensure that everything is covered in the sale.

There is 'no one size fits all' model for the sale of a business, due to the fact that every business and the way that it is run is unique.

Closing

Once the contract is signed and all of the conditions have been complied with, the contract is usually closed with the payment of the purchase price by the buyer to the seller and the transfer of the business to the buyer by the seller. At this point, all of the legal forms to do with the names, telephones, utilities, and so on of the business should be lodged with the respective government departments and suppliers to ensure that the transfer is completed.

This is only a short summary of the considerations to sell a business. As can be seen from this list, it is not a simple process. It is one that takes a considerable amount of work and energy. Throughout the process, it is essential that you engage with and keep abreast of all situations with your attorney, accountant, financial planner, business mentor or coaches, as well as your business broker. All of these consultants are essential to ensure that the business owner achieves the best possible sale price for your business, as well as ensuring that the sale process proceeds smoothly and successfully.

11.3 Considerations about the Sale of Part of the Business

In section 6, I discussed bringing investors into the business. Part of that discussion revolved around the considerations of bringing in an investor and selling part of the business.

This section focuses on selling off a part of a business but not the entire business. The sale of the whole of the business and part of the business are dealt with separately as there are some significant differences between them.

From the Case Files

A classic example of the sale of part of the business is a real estate agent's rent roll. We acted for an agent that had a very large business with a turnover in excess of $5 million per annum and a rent roll of over 800 properties. The owner of the business was tired of dealing with the rent roll side of the business as they did not like dealing with the issues that came about from tenants. They decided that they wanted to sell that part of the business to another agent that was a competitor in their area. As with the majority of real estate agents, they had two aspects of their business; the first is property sales and the second is property management. The management rights to those properties are valuable assets that can be purchased by a third party licensed real estate agent whilst the selling agent retains the sales aspect of their business. The agent was able to sell off that aspect of the business to the competitor real estate agent whilst maintaining their business as a sales agent.

When selling a part of any business, careful consideration needs to be given to how that portion of the business is sold. A contract needs to carefully define what part of the business is being sold as distinct from what is being kept; the contract needs to ensure that there is no room for misunderstanding between the parties as to their ownership rights. It is also critically important to define the restraint of provisions mentioned earlier. Given that the new business owner is only buying a portion of the business, the only part of the business that the seller can be restrained from continuing to trade in is that part of the business which is sold, otherwise, the restraint would not be seen as reasonable and would no doubt be struck out as such.

So for a real estate agency that both sells and leases properties, the seller would be restrained in operating either a rent roll or sales department, depending on which part of the business is sold, but could not be restrained for both (where only a part is sold).

The considerations in selling part of a business are very much dependent on the type of business that is being sold. There will also be different tax consequences when only part of the business is being sold as different rules apply, so it is important that you engage with your advisors early and work through all the issues.

11.4 Listing a Business on a Stock Exchange

The decision to list a company on a Stock Exchange is one that requires careful preparation and consideration on the part of the business owner. The process of listing a company is known as an initial public offering. When a company lists, it is valued and additional shares are issued which can be traded on a Stock Exchange. You may decide to list a company for a number of reasons, such as:

- Positioning the company for expansion into other markets (both nationally and internationally)
- Making it easier to access new capital through public offerings
- Giving shareholders an easier way to sell their shares in the company and having better access to capital management opportunities to pay off debts
- Creating a measurable and transparent valuation for the company
- Giving the company higher credibility as well as greater visibility (given the disclosure requirements for listed companies)

Before listing your company, you need to be 100% positive that you definitely want to do this as not only is the initial public offering process a costly one, but it is also time consuming and one that you cannot afford to get wrong.

It is very important that when you want to list a company on a Stock Exchange that you seek advice from your attorneys, accountants, financial advisors, and other consultants to ensure that it is appropriate to list the company and that the correct steps are taken.

Some of the important positive and negative considerations include:

(a) Positives:

- (i) easier to raise capital through a new share issue
- (ii) easier to sell shares to third parties through the Stock Exchange than trying to sell shares in a private company
- (iii) easier to expand by buying businesses as it is easier to use shares as equity for purchases
- (iv) the company brand is enhanced as a listed company rather than a small to medium private company
- (v) it can be easier to obtain and retain quality team members given the enhanced status as a publicly listed company

(b) Negatives:

- (i) major decisions cannot be made informally but require a longer bureaucratic and less flexible methodology (e.g. board meetings)
- (ii) increased compliance costs, including additional disclosure and accountability requirements
- (iii) higher risk of hostile takeovers as other investors are attracted to buy large stakes in the company
- (iv) the share price is subject to stock market fluctuations beyond the control of company management, which can cause the value of the company to drop against the company's wishes
- (v) loss of privacy as you need to disclose all of the business's information to shareholders

In a broad sense, the steps to list a company on a Stock Exchange are:

- Step one – appoint a broker and attorney to prepare the paperwork for the initial public offering
- Step two – decide on the appropriate exchange terms of the initial public offering and prepare disclosure documents for the initial public offering
- Step three – the broker then organizes for the registration of the company with the Stock Exchange
- Step four – initial discussions begin with potential investors using managed fund investors to test the waters
- Step five – the broker helps to determine the price of the stock
- Step six – the company lists and is traded on the Stock Exchange, with the share price subject to market forces

Before listing, there are a number of matters that you and your management team need to consider, including:

- What gaps are there in the skillset at the management and board level of the company? Can these be resolved with a listed company?
- Is the management of the company ready for the greater disclosure, accountability and transparency requirements after the company is listed?
- Is the company's culture ready to be a listed company?
- Does the company have any issues with tax?
- How will key employees and key customers respond when they learn the news – will they stay on with the company?
- What other initiatives need to be considered (such as other acquisitions) before the company is listed?
- What systems (such as financial, operational and management) need to be improved before the company is listed?
- Are all corporate governance practices properly in place?
- Is the timing right for both the company and the market conditions?

When making the decision to list a company on the Stock Exchange, it is critically important that you obtain advice from all relevant consultants involved in listing the business.

If you do not take the right steps and heed advice during this process, it is more than likely that the listing of the company will be a disaster and cost you dearly without achieving anything.

11.5 Conclusion

This phase is one of the most exciting in the Business Legal Lifecycle as it is here you will see the reward for all of the hard work and patience. Where a business owner follows the Business Legal Lifecycle in full, they will find that their business is properly set up (or close to it) to successfully navigate this phase. Properly handled, this phase will see you reap the benefits of your business. It should occur when the company is at the top of its game, so it achieves the best possible return to you.

Taking the right advice from your consultants will ensure that you can properly navigate this phase and achieve the best return. If you do not take this step, or worse yet this step fails, then you will need to move on to the Retirement phase or, worse yet, the Insolvency/Winding Up phase of the Business Legal Lifecycle.

Dealing with this phase in a careful and methodical way is also important. Rushing through the sale of your business will result in you losing some of the value of the business. You may not be ready to move onto the next phase of Retirement (and may start a new business and Lifecycle all over again) but taking a calm and methodical approach will mean that you have the choice to retire and reap the rewards of all of your hard work and patience or decide upon another course.

QUESTIONS TO ASK BEFORE YOU PROGRESS TO THE NEXT PHASE:

1. Have you put everything in place to be able to sell either the whole or part of your business?
2. Have you engaged a suitable broker to help you sell your business?
3. If you want to list on the Stock Exchange have you engaged the appropriate consultants to assist you in the process?
4. Have you sold your business for the price that you want?

CHAPTER 12

Phase 12 – Retirement

Where a business owner has opted not to sell their business and wants to continue to trade, they will usually want to trade the business until retirement. If you decide to go through this phase of your business, you will need to ensure that you are properly set up for your retirement. The Retirement phase usually occurs after the business has reached and surpassed its peak.

Retirement may not be a result of age; it may also be forced upon you earlier due to illness and are not able to sell the business or because you decided to continue working in the business for a period after you sold it to help with the transition.

Obviously, there are pension plans in many countries but, in most countries, they are not sufficient to allow you to continue to live the lifestyle that you want to in the future. Properly setting up for this phase will ensure that you do not need to rely on such a pension and will be able to fund yourself into the future.

During this phase I will discuss setting yourself up for retirement, different pension options and earnout periods.

Important considerations during this phase are:

- Where will my income come from after I retire?
- What will happen to my business when I retire?
- Is there an opportunity to sell the business at this point?
- Do I need to revisit an earlier phase of the Business Legal Lifecycle?

Dangerous considerations during this phase are:

- I don't need to do anything to set myself up for retirement
- It will just work out
- I do not want to think about retirement

12.1 Setting Up for Retirement

Earlier, I discussed the advantages of investing profits in income generating assets (see section 9). One of the reasons behind such an investment was to allow you to retire and continue funding the lifestyle that you deserve. You should seek advice from a qualified professional financial planner to help them plan their retirement and review crucial questions such as (this list is not exhaustive):

(a) What income do you require to be able to live comfortably in your retirement?

(b) What risks are you willing to take with your investments to increase your potential return?

(c) What assets do you currently own and what income do they generate?

(d) What assets do you need to acquire to generate the income that you need to retire comfortably?

There are many other considerations that are unique to each person's circumstances. The best advice I can give you is to seek the advice of a qualified financial planner, your attorney and your accountant and collectively plan out your retirement strategy. There are many circumstances where clients have taken advice from a financial planner and set themselves up for retirement.

From the Case Files

An example of this was a client who, at the age of 40, realized that she had not put any plans in place for her retirement. She had operated a manufacturing business producing furniture for over 20 years and had made a nice profit along the way. However, she had spent the majority of her profits on consumable products and overseas holidays and did not have significant savings to be able to fund her retirement. She sought advice from a financial planner to assist with setting up a plan to try to save enough money to help her retire. She started to invest the profits from her business into investments that derived her income. This meant that by the time she turned 55 she was able to comfortably retire.

12.2 Retirement Plans

A retirement plan allows individuals to save money for their retirement. In some countries there are mandatory retirement plans. In the United States participation in retirement plans is usually voluntary. There are a variety of retirement savings accounts, including:

(a) Individual Retirement Arrangements (IRAs)

(b) Roth IRAs

(c) 401(k) Plans

(d) 403(b) Plans

(e) SIMPLE IRA Plans (Savings Incentive Match Plans for Employees)

(f) Simplified Employee Pension (SEP) Plans

(g) Salary Reduction Simplified Employee Pension (SARSEP) Plans

(h) Payroll Deduction IRAs

(i) Profit-Sharing Plans

(j) Defined Benefit Plans

(k) Money Purchase Plans

(l) Employee Stock Ownership Plans (ESOPs)

(m) Governmental Plans

(n) 457 Plans

It is outside the scope of this book to explain each one in detail. If you want further advice on which is right for you and/or your team you should consult your financial planner.

Before establishing a retirement plan, you need to understand the advantages and drawbacks of each plan in light of when you plan to retire. You need to carefully consider your position and seek advice from all of your advisors about what the best retirement plan is for you.

12.3 Earnout Periods

Often in the sale phase of a business, you may decide that you want to continue working in the business during an earnout period and you can also consider not selling all of the business assets. From the seller's perspective, a earnout is not something that they particularly may want as it is often used by the buyer to either reduce the purchase price or stage payments for it.

The main drawback with this type of arrangement is that the retiring business owner is at the mercy of the new business owner, the terms of the earnout agreement and the ongoing successful operation of the business before they receive their profits. The best way to avoid an earnout is to have a business that has been developed through the Business Legal Lifecycle, which will ensure that it is a properly set up and saleable business, and that you do not have to honor an earnout period for the business as the buyer will be able to operate the business with you.

From the Case Files

An example of where this did not work was a business owner who owned a printing business. The business had been operating for over 30 years and the owner had originally bought it from the original founder some 20 years beforehand. Even with the significant challenges that printing businesses faced in recent years, this business was making a nice profit for the business owner to be able to live comfortably. A buyer approached the business owner with a view to being able to work with the business owner to increase the profitability of the business and then buy the business owner out for a more significant amount of money than the business was worth at that time. However, the new owner wanted the business owner to continue working in the business, increase the business and its profitability before being paid a price for the business. The business did not become more profitable and the buyer was shown to have no business acumen. The once profitable printing business was making the same mistakes that a lot of its competitors were making and was not innovating as required to beat the downturn in the printing industry. The business ended up folding with large debts and the client was left with nothing from the business that they had operated for 20 years.

You may also decide you don't want to sell all of the business assets and want to retain some to generate a future income. A prime example is intellectual property, which you can license to generate an income after you retire. As with any investment, there is a risk in retaining ownership of part of the business.

Additionally, if you retain part of the assets, the sale price of the business will be lower. As discussed in section 11, it is important that any sale of whole or part of your business proceeds with the right advice.

From the Case Files

Of course earnout periods work as long as the goals are realistic and achievable. An example of this was an accountancy business. The client sold his business to an employee who had worked in the business for some time. The client was able to maintain and slightly increase the business during his earnout period meaning that the seller was paid a premium for the business and the buyer was left with a strong and profitable business that continued to trade successfully for many years.

12.4 Conclusion

The decision to retire is one of the biggest that you will make during the Business Legal Lifecycle. Taking care of all of the aspects of the business and ensuring that you can comfortably retire is an important consideration for you to make. As I said earlier, the pension alone is generally insufficient to allow you to properly retire. Therefore, it is critical that you take the advice of your consultants to ensure that you can properly navigate your way through this phase to allow you to live the lifestyle that you want. Properly navigating your way through this phase will mean that you are set up for the future and the negative effects of the final phase, Insolvency/Winding Up, will not impact on you too greatly.

QUESTIONS TO ASK BEFORE YOU PROGRESS TO THE NEXT PHASE:

1. Do you have enough passive income to fund your retirement?
2. Have you determined what will happen to your business when you retire?
3. Is there an opportunity to sell the business at this point and do you need to revisit an earlier phase of the Business Legal Lifecycle?

CHAPTER 13
Phase 13 – Insolvency/Winding Up

The Insolvency/Winding Up phase is the last phase and completes the Business Legal Lifecycle, which means that the business has come to an end. Some business owners will never get to this point as they may retire or sell their business before they get to this phase. However, more often than not, the vehicle that operates the business will need to go through this process once the business is sold to ensure that all of the funds and obligations are properly dealt with from a legal and tax perspective.

For this reason, this phase is not necessarily a negative one and, properly managed, you can avoid some of the common pitfalls. If a business reaches this phase without the opportunity to go through the preceding phases of the Business Legal Lifecycle, then something has gone terribly wrong and the previous phases were not properly completed.

By successfully navigating your way through this phase you will come through to the other side and will be able to start a new business and go through the Business Legal Lifecycle all over again. Failing this phase can cause significant costs and problems for you in the future. Obtaining the right advice during this phase is critical to ensure that this does not happen.

In this phase I will discuss the consequences of insolvency, winding up and bankruptcy to give you an idea of what you could be dealing with.

Important considerations during this phase are:

- Do I want to prevent insolvency?
- If so, what can be done to prevent insolvency?
- What are the consequences to my business if I prevent insolvency?
- How can I deal with those issues?
- Am I comfortable with my creditors not being paid?
- Is there any way that I can deal with creditors moving forward?

Dangerous considerations during this phase are:

- I do not need advice – I can do this myself
- If I do not do anything, then it will all go away
- The other side have been mean to me so I am not going to pay their debts
- I will not pay them out of principle

13.1 Insolvency

There are a number of different legal definitions of the term 'insolvency' but I think the best definition of the term is that when a company or a person is not able to pay its debts as and when they are due and payable, then the company or the person is insolvent.

If a company or a person has lots of debts, however, but they are not due and payable at a particular point in time but at some time in the future, they are not insolvent. This means that a debt-ridden company or person may be able to continue trading and be able to raise the funds to pay their debts in due course. However, if that same company or person cannot pay all of their debts as they fall due and owing, the company or person will be insolvent. In practical terms, determining when a company is solvent and insolvent is not a precise science. There are many different tests including the cash flow test and the balance sheet test. The cash flow test is essentially what I have discussed above as it determines if a company is able to continue to pay its debts. The balance sheet test looks at a company's balance sheet and determines its ability to collect money, and whether it will be enough to pay its creditors in full.

If you are concerned that your business may be insolvent, you should immediately obtain advice from your legal and financial advisors and, if applicable, an insolvency professional to determine whether or not your business is insolvent. Taking early action can help prevent larger problems from developing and allows you an opportunity to manage, as best you can, the insolvency process.

From the Case Files

An example of this difficulty was where a client operating a large steel post manufacturing firm came to me showing their profit on paper to be considerable but with little cash in the bank account. The business was making a great profit but they were not generating the operating cash flow that they needed to survive as they did not have any debt collection procedures in place. This meant that the client thought that everything was going well but that the business was spending more money than the cash it was getting in. The business had so many creditors that would not wait for payment that the company was deemed insolvent because it could not pay its debts. One creditor would not wait for payment and wound up the company. This meant that the business ended abruptly despite being profitable on paper. The company's employees lost their jobs and the customers lost all of the work that they had been waiting for from the business as it simply ceased trading and the half-finished items were sold as scrap metal.

13.2 Winding Up

When a company is insolvent, it can be wound up, which involves a liquidator being appointed to control and finalize the company (the management or creditors of a company may decide to appoint an administrator and go into administration first if there is a chance of the business being rescued and/or the company's debts are more likely to be paid off if the company can continue temporarily as a going concern). The actual process of winding up involves all of the assets of the company being sold, and the remaining money being used to pay off the remaining debts. In the rare event that there are additional funds, the money can be distributed to shareholders. Once this process is completed, the company is then deregistered or struck off from the register of companies and no longer exists.

A company can be wound up under a variety of circumstances, but the more common instances are:

(a) where a company owes a debt and will not (or cannot) pay it, the unpaid creditors can apply to the courts to have that company wound up

(b) in some circumstances where the directors of the company determine that it cannot pay its debts, the directors can seek to appoint a liquidator to wind up the company

(c) in some circumstances the shareholders of the company can decide that the company does not have the funds to continue trading and pay its debts and seek to appoint a liquidator to wind up the company

A liquidator is an independent third party, often with an accounting background, who manages the affairs of the company to wind the company up. Before the winding up process commences, the company can also have administrators appointed (by its directors, shareholders or creditors) to analyze the company's financial position and attempt to restructure the company or trade it out of difficulty.

Strict rules apply in the event of the winding up of a company. Once a liquidator is appointed, the directors of the company lose their control over the company and the liquidator assumes the responsibility and control over the company's operational matters.

Often, the debts of the company are canceled, and the directors can even be banned from managing companies for a number of years (depending on the severity of their actions).

This section is only a very brief overview of the winding up process and the effect that such a decision has on a company. Where you are subject to such a decision you should obtain advice from your attorney, accountant and other advisors to ensure that the debts are fairly dealt with and the process is managed properly.

13.3 Bankruptcy

When an individual is insolvent, they can be declared bankrupt. There are two ways this can happen:

- a person can declare themselves bankrupt or
- a person's creditors can apply to court to have the person declared bankrupt

When a person is bankrupted they have an order made against their estate. This bankruptcy order has the effect of taking all of the assets of the person, which are then sold and used to pay the debts of the individual.

Most of the debts that the person owes are compromised (although there are some exceptions to that rule; often government fines are not compromised) and the person will be bankrupted for a mandatory period of time (this is dependent on the type of bankruptcy) and the information on the person's credit report lasts for 7 to 10 years.

(a) **If a person becomes bankrupt what debts form part of their bankrupt estate?**

When a person is declared bankrupt, they are obliged to complete a 'Statement of Affairs'. The majority of debts are proved as valid (provable debts) in bankruptcy; however, a number of government-imposed expenses are not provable such as:

(i) debts that a person incurs after the date of bankruptcy

(ii) spousal maintenance

(iii) child support

(iv) debts incurred by fraud

When a bankrupt is discharged from bankruptcy, they will be released from provable debts; however, the debts listed above will still be owed by the bankrupt. Any debts of secured creditors (this means that the creditor has a right to recover a person's physical asset such as a mortgage of a person's home) are not affected by a person's bankruptcy. The secured creditor can enforce their rights against the property, sell the property and then become an unsecured creditor of the bankrupt estate for any shortfall.

Unsecured creditors generally do not have the right to repossess goods to sell them, but may receive a partial payment based on the debts that the bankrupt person owes. Any debts that a bankrupt person incurs after they are declared bankrupt are debts that the bankrupt person is personally responsible to repay and do not form part of the estate.

(b) **What assets can a bankrupt person keep?**

A bankrupt person will generally be entitled to retain their personal belongings but not assets. An asset is anything that can be owned that is not a personal belonging and includes real property, chattels or possessions. Generally, a bankrupt person's reasonably necessary household items, furniture and personal effects are not assets that form part of the bankrupt estate. A bankrupt person may also be able to keep tools that they use to earn an income, as well as vehicles (including cars or motorbikes) so long as certain criteria are met.

A person's residence forms part of their bankrupt estate and is not protected property. If the house is mortgaged there are a variety of options that can be used to protect the house but usually the mortgagee of the property will sell it to settle the mortgage owed by the bankrupt person.

(c) **Does bankruptcy affect a person's employment?**

Generally, bankruptcy does not prevent a person from working but a number of industries may be affected by a person being declared bankrupt. If the bankrupt person is engaged in particular trades or professions, there may be certain restrictions imposed by their professional organization or government legislation and rules. For example, if you become bankrupt often it is difficult for you to become an attorney, bank manager or financial advisor. You also need to be aware that a bankrupt is allowed to earn a certain amount of money before they must give a percentage of their earnings to their bankruptcy trustee.

This is a brief overview of the bankruptcy process and is designed to be read as a starting point. When dealing with these issues, you should seek the advice of your attorney, accountant, financial consultants and any business mentors to ensure that you can properly navigate your way through this process in a controlled and proper way.

13.4 Dissolution

Where your business was operated through a company when it ceases to operate, you can also elect to dissolve the company. Dissolution means that the company is removed from the register of active companies and ceases to operate as a separate legal entity. This is the effect of a liquidation of a company but you can also choose to do this voluntarily if and when the business meets certain criteria. Dissolution is not a simple process and you need to ensure that you have the advice of your accountants, attorneys and financial advisors to ensure that it is done correctly and that no loose ends remain.

13.5 Conclusion

Understanding the rules and regulations around insolvency is important but they are complicated. No two insolvencies are ever the same, and the advice you receive and action you need to take will be specific to your particular circumstances. It is important that, if you are facing bankruptcy or insolvency, you do not obtain 'barbecue advice' from your friends but specialist advice from professionals such as attorneys, accountants and financial consultants who specialize in these areas, to prevent your situation from becoming worse or further issues from arising in the future as a result of this process.

From the Case Files

An example of this is a situation where a business owner had some large debts that he had amassed. The business that he operated was a large construction company with a significant turnover of over $5 million but the owner was not able to pay all of the debts that were due for the business. He received 'barbecue advice' to the effect that he should simply declare himself bankrupt or let his creditors do it for him so that he would not have to pay the debt. The business owner owed approximately $600,000.00 in debts and had over $2 million worth of assets in his own name. If he had gone down the bankruptcy path, he would have lost most of the $2 million of assets and would not have had anything to show for his hard work as a business owner for many years. It was not until he received the right advice that he was able to realize that declaring bankruptcy was not the right path and that would have disastrous consequence for him and his assets. Finally given the right advice, the business owner borrowed enough money against his assets to pay the debts that he owed. As a result of our advice he retained his assets and business and was able to keep his lifestyle going the way he wanted to.

WHERE TO FROM HERE?

1. Is insolvency necessary or is there another path?
2. Have you retired?
3. If you do not want to retire then you need to start from the beginning of the Business Legal Lifecycle all over again with a new business or go and work for someone.

Conclusion

In business you are always learning new systems, procedures and methodologies. This book is all about educating you on the different aspects of your business and when legal processes and considerations should be implemented. The main reason that I wrote this book and developed the Business Legal Lifecycle was to share my experience as a business owner and an attorney. We built our law firm on the principle of 'Solutions for a Better Life' and all of the work we do is geared towards that goal.

Understanding the Business Legal Lifecycle is not the end point for any business owner; it is the beginning of how to operate your business, how to grow your business and how to prepare for your future. It is critical that you understand the different phases and times when different legal processes should be followed. It is also critical that you have a basic understanding of a number of legal concepts when in business. I hope that you have appreciated the explanations that I have given in this book and that it gives you, as a business owner, a greater understanding of the legal processes involved in operating a business.

I have used many examples and case studies in this book to illustrate how legal processes work and why they are important. You may find these examples similar to your own experiences or you may find that when you are faced with a similar situation, you can identify a potential problem and fix it before it becomes an issue. No two situations are ever exactly the same but you need to know when to take action at the appropriate time. This will prevent you from continually treading water or, worse yet, being swept away when problems occur.

It is important to remember that in business you will face tough times; that is the nature of business and it is entirely normal. It is *how* you deal with those problems that will determine how successful you are in the future. I also encourage you to read all you can and take in as much advice (but not 'barbecue advice'!) as you can in relation to operating your business. Do not implement everything you read and hear; consider your options and, if you are not sure of which way to go, it is probably best to take the course of a trusted advisor. Running a business is a rewarding endeavor and is something that I am very glad I have been able to participate in.

As you will have gathered from this book it is important that throughout the Business Legal Lifecycle you obtain advice from the right consultants at the right time.

Often attorneys or accountants will try to do too much, or they will not allow the other consultants to do their job. I have tried to also point out the various types of consultants that I recommend that business owners engage with at different times in their business.

I wish you the best of luck in your journey in business and through the Business Legal Lifecycle. If you have any questions, then please feel free to email me at lifecycle@jeremystreten.com.

www.ingramcontent.com/pod-product-compliance
Lightning Source LLC
Chambersburg PA
CBHW051125091125
35079CB00056B/4150
9781925921205